The memoir genre is loaded with tellings by survivors of family dysfunction. This one is a love letter. *Mother of the Child* captures how memory functions as an aspect of the soul. It is a transparent model of the examined life, of family bonds – within and without.

— **Wayne Grogan, author, Ned Kelly Award winner**

Jill Forster is a seriously gifted 'poetic prose' author who has a mastery of language and expression and literature. This is an extraordinary family memoir, full of historical recollections that took me back to my own childhood.

— **Gary Martin, publisher, Deep Line Books**

A laser-like focus on things that are not only nostalgia triggers, but are in fact full of symbolism. I particularly liked the way the narrative and the poems fitted together, erudite and deceptively simple. It put me in mind of Tim Winton's *Island Home* and the English writer Ted Walker's *The High Path*.

— **Phil Donnelly, poet and critic**

Praise for *Mother of the Child*

Magically compelling, honest and insightful, *Mother of the Child* takes the reader through a beautiful and authentic journey of an Australian woman's life from the mid-20th century, so real and resonant that the reader can smell the soup on the stove, hear the cockatoos screeching, taste the sea salt on the beach towels and see the bobby pins on the dressing table. It is at the same time a monument to a life that has filled with love of family, the Australian landscape and life itself, with all of its joy and injustices, balanced beautifully but without undue sentimentality, with timeless poetry, remnants of philosophy and enduring gratefulness for a mother's gift of life and love. Somewhat unexpectedly, along the way it helps to nurture and heal those who have lost and need to live again.
— **Kaaren Koomen AM, Director, Governmental & Regulatory Affairs, IBM Australia & New Zealand**

Mother of the Child is a poetic reflection of the wonder and innocence of childhood and an elegy for a simpler time.
— **Nicki Roller, Deputy Head of Production, SBS**

Part prose, part poetry, part memoir, part conversation with the past, *Mother of the Child* is Jill Forster's evocation of her relationship with her mother and her relationship with herself. Think of this as a literary photo album where words replace pictures. What Forster shows us is that every small observation is significant, that there is meaning in everything in this elegiac narrative of a time not quite lost.
— **Clare Calvet, ABC Radio reviewer for 25 years**

An extended and intensely lyrical poem, in prose and verse, as well as being a meditation on childhood memories and the experience of parenting. The unforgotten details of one particular childhood take on universality as they are evoked in richly expressive and rhythmic language, bringing back to life 'that leap of joy like a fat raisin squelching with buttered glee, drunk on liquid laughter'. While at the end of the book there is sadness, it only comes at the end of a narrative bursting with that buttery, liquid joy.

— **Jamie Grant, literary critic and author**

This book is a series of love letters to the author's mother and to motherhood; to growing up in Australia and to memory itself. It is superbly written, absorbing the reader instantly in a time and place that is terribly familiar, yet also unique to the author's experience. The stories are of joy and of terrible grief, but most of all this is a book about love. Love of family, love of nature and place, and most of all the incomparable and unique love a mother provides to her children and the love she receives in return. I heartily recommend this beautiful book.

— **Verity Firth, Executive Director Social Justice, University of Technology Sydney, and former New South Wales parliamentarian**

Evocative and surreal and somehow very familiar. This book is a treasure trove of beautifully crafted word paintings. Intriguing descriptions of time and place tumble off the page, each one as cleverly written as the next. This story feels like you've lived it yourself, such is the deftness and depth of the writing.

— **Jenny Morris, singer-songwriter, OAM, MNZM**

MOTHER OF THE CHILD

A Memoir within a Memoir

JILL FORSTER

BY THE SAME AUTHOR

HONEYED RAMBLINGS

LULLABIES

THINK ABOUT CREATIVITY

THINK ABOUT MENTORING

JILL FORSTER

With a PhD in educational psychology and curriculum, Jill Forster has worked as an independent consultant, university lecturer and secondary school teacher, and has continued to run creative writing workshops and write freelance.

Since completing *Mother of the Child*, Jill has been collaborating in an art and poetry project, written more than 100 collected poems, and has a set of "short stories" underway. Her professional articles appear in peer-reviewed journals and research textbooks on the topics of creative thinking and (under) achievement. Her individual poems have been published in collations such as a chapbook (NSW Government Arts Council grant), magazines and online (for the National Library and Royal Botanic Gardens), and her other published writings include the books *Think about Creativity, Think about Mentoring*, and two poetry books: *Lullabies* and *Honeyed Ramblings*.

Published by ORiGiN™ IMPRiNT 2020
www.originimprint.com

Copyright © Jill Forster 2019

Jill Forster asserts the moral right to be identified as the author of this work.
All rights reserved. Apart from any fair dealing for the purposes of study, research, criticism, review, or as otherwise permitted under the Copyright Act, no part of this publication may be reproduced or transmitted in any form or by any means, electrical or mechanical, including photocopying, recording, or by any information storage or retrieval system, without permission in writing from the publisher.

Typeset by Amber Quin

 A catalogue record for this book is available from the National Library of Australia

Forster, Jill
Mother of the Child
ISBN: 978-0-6485874-1-5

Printed and bound in Australia

ORiGiN™ IMPRiNT
PO Box 1235
QVB Post Office
NSW 1230 Australia

ACKNOWLEDGEMENTS

To my family – for their love and nurturing, my heartfelt thanks. Because of them the world is lit up, and amazing memories keep spindrifting in.

For Philip Walker's embrace of my writing I am very grateful and to all his team for their efforts – including Philip Mortlock, Amber Quin and Nick Young. Gratitude also to publicist Gary Martin who has given so much support and careful consideration. To friend and editor Margaret McKay huge thanks for her selfless and patient editing.

With my friends and the friendship they offer I am blessed. Their smiles and hugs and interest are always appreciated.

It is truly humbling to hear readers' generous reactions to my words when they strike a chord, trigger a memory, a set of sounds or images they especially enjoyed, a poem that for them was apt. It is for these connections to others' thoughts that I love to write.

DEDICATION

To all nurturers and to all those in need of nurturing.

You must live in the present, launch yourself on every wave, find your eternity in each moment.
— Thoreau

FRAGMENTS

REFLECTIONS within REFLECTIONS	1
SWEETNESS and LIGHT	5
Faith and Fairies and Pixie-lit Lanterns	10
Cocoons and Silk	17
Bliss, Bees and Butterflies	19
Humming and Hydrangeas	24
Backyard or Beyond - rhus trees and rhubarb	25
Fair and Foul Play	29
Pea-shelling in the afternoon	32
Lemon-squeezing and Lighting Candles	35
School Days – milk,	
marbles and Mercurochrome	37
Ritual and Routine – tea and truth	40
Home and Hearth	44
SPOTLIGHT on HEATHER:	
HERITAGE, HISTORY and HOPES	49
Inventions and Inventiveness	52
War and Wisdom, Smoke and Mirrors	56
Doors Opening and Closing	59
Fashion and Frivolity	62
Landscape and Lustre	65
Castles and Creeks	71
Cockatoos and Sapphires	73
Sanskrit and Sails	81
Music and Musings and Movie stars	86

Melodies and Makin' Whoopee	89
Posies, Peonies and Poppies	92
Pearls and Perfumes, Pom-poms and Pomp	95
Quirks, Quality and the Quaint	99
Fences and Faraway	104
Ghosts and Angels	107
Thyme and Timelessness	112
Marmalade and Slow Motion	116
FADE to GREY	**121**
Lights Low	125
Fragile Faith	130
Off Balance – bickering and bombings	134
Naïveté and Nuances	137
Icons and Incongruities	140
Grace, Gratitude and Grit	143
Turning Tide	146
From Hula Hoops to Hipsters	150
Flux	155
Aspro and Lymphoma, Hiccups and Oesophaguses	157
Time traveller and Time-pieces	163

REFLECTIONS WITHIN REFLECTIONS

Long lolling days. Through the summers in the 1960s, under the surf-green and white concentric circles of the beach umbrella secured deeply in the sand, there sat my parents, two older brothers and I, watching and reading the waves. On some days trailing across the sand hills, nuns in their black habits, ant-lined across the dunes – black figures in rows, they sank into the gold grit.

Is my preoccupation with this random scene because my mother delighted so much to see them? Is my reflection filtered through my mother's reflections or hers through mine? Or does it chime with my sense of awe at the coming together of the congruous and the incongruous, something beyond our clear comprehension, a link between earthbound and ethereal, the ground and the sky. Like a sandpiper that has flown in and is now pecking at the sandy particles underfoot and between the toes, there's something about finding our eternity in a grain of sand.

Reflecting on my mother's life is like looking out on a wistful wave of times gone by. We're riding the incoming swell, yet detached from the rolling fall of memories shared on the seemingly endless tide of a person's life as it is lived. It is about the ways in which we look for and embrace opportunity, we cope with or succumb to distress, or learn to seek out what will soothe our longings. We all in some measure chase our faraway.

It is that sense of something that is outside of ourselves, and yet in its pursuit makes us who we are. This is where the normal, the infinitely normal, becomes unique.

Infinitely normal

But for her smile,
Her laugh
From within
From way back
When her world was
Full of joy and promise…
It never kept.

In its way this memoir within a memoir, smelted and annealed through poetry, is written to represent that of many a mother who has imparted wisdom gleaned from a way of seeing through her own particular lens on life. These sung vignettes of my mother's lived experiences might strike a chord that can come from hearing familiar notes, and give voice on behalf of another whose own voice was sometimes faint and in need of a megaphone.

Along the arc of memories – from sweet to sad, and light to shade – there are my own reflections on the wash of childhood days that started with the dawn cooing of doves outside our bedroom windows, and closed after the backyard cricket, cowboys and Indians, and baths full of soap suds. There are outlines of my mother's early days, her meeting my father and their wartime selves, into parenthood with its joys and certainly with its grief, when the days drifted into the less quiet days of adolescent conflict and the awakening of adult responsibilities and decisions. All the fragments are lit up through my mother's gaze.

Like light on the white sun-caught sails of a lone boat on the open sea, these words that follow will spotlight some moments and recollections. But they are simply glimpses and so, no sooner than the sail is lit up, its form fades into the background sky and the sun's glow escapes out of focus, blending into the horizon.

On Reflection

Take her to the beyond
To see the fairy pond
And spy on her reflection
The child and woman in introspection.

SWEETNESS AND LIGHT

La lune ne garde aucune rancune.
(The moon bears no grudge.)

— T.S. Eliot

It's January again and here we are in the hot old Vauxhall – three children across the backseat, me in the middle – driving for a couple of hours around the many bends well before the road was upgraded to a freeway. The bellbirds would send a clear chime across the valley as if to alert us that we were nearly there. Close to the turn-off at the three ways fork we would stop to pick up fresh corncobs and an enormous cool-skinned watermelon which it was my job to keep on my lap until we got there.

We stayed in a beach cottage with a tank for collecting rainwater that had to be boiled for drinking, and we squealed when we turned on the tap and saw baby tadpoles. We would often seek out the minuscule pink frogs that camouflaged their existence on rain-soaked leaves and croaked their incessant incantation in the echoing bathroom pipes. And there was the rich milk from local cows and in the neck of the milk bottle, clotted cream so thick it would stick in our throats. Outside the window in the bottlebrush bushes, the throat of the wattle bird wobbled, with its loud, distinctive ricochets of clicks, while its head pulled in to the subdued feathers of its speckled chest.

Still I can smell the banksia trees, still I can see the rickety steps, and the big old brown suitcase that my mother packed with clothes for the whole family. A long sausage bag my father had used in the army was stuffed with bath and beach towels and bed-linen for the two weeks. No washing machine, no drinkable tap water, no electricity without coins in the meter. But for my mother, these holidays and their nostalgia were important. Shining on our sea-sung sleep was the enormous moon which never did bear a grudge from one innocent day to the next. Across the horizon she simply murmured her way into our sight, a round miracle of milk on ink.

Tide charts, winds, shells and bluebottles were our preoccupations. We surfed and rolled down sand hills for most of the day, and learned to swim in the quiet estuary lake. Each day when it was time for lunch we would hotfoot it back over the scorching sand and continue down the dirt road to the post-office. There the postmistress sold fat loaves of very fresh bread that we took home for lunch and topped with ham and cheese, followed by chunks of watermelon eaten in the backyard so we could spit out the pips onto the soil. Simple days.

Immutable Mollusc

Leave it resting
to see if it's still here
on our return.
Will it wait an eternity?
the wash and tide
dissolving.

When a summer afternoon clouded over, instead of surfing, we went wandering along the beach finding purple-shelled pippis. My mother taught us to watch the horizon for white horses in their infinite race to the shore, their foaming manes flying out as they rode in across the dark celadon seas.

There beyond the breakers, below the overcast sky, that hung low over the ocean, we often saw a shark's fin. Mystery, a sense of treachery and awe became a part of our seaside psyche – there were things bigger than us and our small understanding.

On other sun-filled days we saw that lone, lone white sail making progress across the dark disturbed sea, the determined lit-up sail listing in its effort to arrive, all the while soaking in the sun's rays gleaming. It was as if a force had intervened and was deciding its tack, enlightening its resolve, sending it to a faraway world, some white sail in Flaubert's mists of the horizon. The spindrift of those days blows in much more than memories of the cresting waves in the wind.

She drifted in like the floss on a fairy

Born under a waxing white moon
She danced to an optimistic tune.
With her whole sweet self she speaks,
As a butterfly kissing our cheeks.

In whispers across the sea
She is simply happy to be.
Family cobweb's smiling ties
Light up like dancing fireflies.
She headed out to brave the wondrous world
Around her summer's salt gossamers swirled.
Her wings touched down low and tipped the froth,
Furred and fragile as a moth.

She flew light and free as thistledown
Floating along after gold sundown.
Innocent babe yet her timing quite sophisticated
With evening light her rhythms syncopated.

Squirming and blanket jiving
With love's tunes she's thriving.
Bobbing like a hungry pigeon
Forthright and fulsome.

With cherished embrace and cuddles
She will escape all sorts of muddles.
Her mother and father as her compass,
Steering her through tears and ruckus.

One day she will want to set sail
Maybe at dawn's calm, maybe in a gale.
She will turn her own true rudder,
Set off with a frisson, a thrill, a grinning shudder.

Then she will throw off the bowlines
Follow her own signs.
Catch the winds in her sails,
Exploring life's mystery trails.
Her world full of conundrums and wonder
She will not fear the dark nor the thunder.
Wander the far and the not-so-far.
Gaze long at every blessing's star.

Faith and Fairies and Pixie-lit Lanterns

Come Fairies, take me out of this dull world, for I would ride with you upon the wind and dance upon the mountains like a flame!

— William Butler Yeats

Memories return from the murmurings of other days. The air of childhood was often filled with whispers of fairies among the she-oaks down the bush where we played for hours and hours, curious as mangrove crabs, until hunger and a fear of the dark to come drove us home. The bush, our second backyard garden, was peopled with banksia men and gum nut babies from the May Gibbs children's stories of *Snugglepot and Cuddlepie,* written a hundred years ago. I can see those banksia men glowering, scowling, the gnarled seed pods cracked open into rough brown grimaces. In the trees the cicadas whir; the bee rests in the full sun that smelts the gold on its wings glinting, and overhead the magpie. On the banksia tree, leaves serrated like the marks of her pinking shears, my mother would etch messages to me from the fairies.

Was my love of fantasy fanned by my mother's need for escape, was it her love too? Certainly, one reinforced the other. Was it her clinging onto her own childhood's innocence, this cocooning in the silken mirth of childhood? Was it her longing to be outside of herself, to be beyond family flaws and foibles? Did she write fairy letters and make bramble-berry fairy wings just for me? Dancing, as if with the grace and light of the sugar plum fairy, I'd revel in tutus and dress-up costumes and dream with Pookie the winged rabbit in sandcastles shining with pixie-lit lanterns and glistening sandcastles – the surreal and real in one – there was a veritable alchemy of childhood enchantment. My imagination flew.

A winter's morning would start with more naïve fiction, as Gary O'Callaghan's character of Sammy Sparrow arrived in his helicopter on radio waves of 2UE – every day at the same time. We would all faithfully listen up as if this were the truth, and news stories were real. But out the window in the backyard, the mysterious Jack Frost had white-iced the glassy grass spikes with his shiny finger-tips.

In later childhood and adolescence, and then into adult years, more fantasies permeated the everyday. The quest of faith and fairy was reinforced in the Morgan le Fay Arthurian legends. We saw in the movie *Camelot* and in Tennyson's poem the pre-Raphaelite beauty of the *Lady of Shalott* in her grey castle tower weaving "magic sights", seen only in her mirror's reflections. Not for us, though, any fear of a curse in real life. There were the glistening icicled fingertips of the snow queen, and the spells of Merlin the magician. As though we were the Hans Christian Anderson mermaids, we floated across the waves and draped ourselves in seaweed, like Prufrock's "sea-girls", as we were to read later, who were singing their alluring song and "combing the white hair of the waves blown back."

All these characters across our childhood – Celts, sorcerers, summer nights' dreams, the unicorn, that "ancient mystic legend" of the Cluny medieval tapestries. The poet Rilke described the unicorn as something unreal, but believe in it and it might just dance in the "tranquil gaze of light." Or does it just stand for something non-existent, like boxing at shadows or tilting at windmills? Were they just fabulous monsters as Alice in Wonderland had thought, or lessons for real life? All this not far removed from the days that my mother had spent listening to her Irish grandmother's tales about the fairies and the idea that people could be fey, having that sixth sense that gave them a special insight into the inexplicable.

Meandering with the fearlessness of Daedalus, I find my way piecing together snippets of clues in the maze of my mother's life, as collected from my childhood, stepping inside the myths and legends. She had treasured a school academic prize, an elegant black and gold covered book with classical black and white photographs of Greek gods and goddesses. There was the goddess Ariadne who punished Arachne's long spindling fingers turning them to spider legs. And under the moon "like a ghostly galleon tossed upon cloudy seas" (Alfred Noyes), we would recall tales of Diana the moon goddess. Whether we have been suspended in time while watching a bird in flight or been lured by the moon's light as the Italian writer, Giacomo Leopardi thought, there we stay spellbound with a sense of unattainability, enchanted nevertheless:

> What are you doing moon there in the sky?
> Tell me silent moon, what?
> You rise in the evening, and pass by,
> Pondering wastelands. Then you set.

Winter Solstice

In our hibernal state
through the midwinter daylight,
in the longest night lying low,
filtered in our down-turned hemisphere,
we make less haste to face the day,
and the sun conspires in the trickery,
a sleight of hand
steals our light,
our two hemispheres in opposite directions,
off-centred,
all may not be as it seems,
the clock does not tell the sun time truth;
along the earthly axis
we're tilting at windmills.

So our hours were filled with the sounds of legends and lullabies. Pictures in hard-spined books were pored over hour after sweet hour, and coloured pencils were the cutting edge technology of the day. Nursery rhymes filled our heads and hearts that sang with fulsome effort, with no intention other than to do what was called for by an unquestioned authority, respected and knowing, and rules always followed. Except for the fascination of the marcasite watch on the teacher's wrist and her petticoats glimpsed during our floor time songs, everything was as normal as the bloomers we wore while we played on the jungle gym.

Owl and the Banksia Man went to the mountains
In a beautiful pumpkin carriage
They took some mouse and plenty of nous
Wrapped up in a promise of marriage.
They danced in the apple orchard
And tossed the sweet pink ladies
They bought some pie and saw Piglet fly
And strummed our tunes on ukuleles.

While still with the innocence of an unknowing child though, the place where I would often linger was in my mother's room as she got ready to go out. She might have just had her hair in rollers, and dried under a portable Sunbeam hairdryer with a plastic cap. And then she covered her hair in a fairy-printed scarf. It was intriguing for a child to see some of the things that were part of a woman's adult world, like her bed jackets in exquisite silk and muslin, her ironed lace handkerchiefs she kept in an embroidered handkerchief sachet in her dressing table drawer, her hats in a round brown leather hatbox with a midnight-blue ruched silk lining.

In her very own space at her dressing-table, with its concertina mirror three-sided and edged with bezelled glass, was a crystal tray. There she had her heavy bristle hairbrush, a solid piece that stood for nurturing, this time for herself. She even loved to have her hair brushed as though she were again the child. Thick dark brown curly hair, long, with a swept back wave at the front in a mini pompadour held with bobby pins, was the style my mother wore when first married. By the time she had three children she had lopped off her hair to a neat and practical bob.

Also on the crystal tray was a crystal powder bowl where she kept safety pins – lots of those, just in case – brooches and eyebrow tweezers, essential to her sense of good grooming. And there was her jar of cold cream to smooth off the day's dust and nourish the skin smoothed over with "honey beige" liquid foundation and rouge. With these she would prepare her presentable herself.

In the subdued lighting of the art deco lamp with a base in the form of a female figure somewhere between a movie star and a siren fairy, picking up her crystal-backed mirror from the dressing table, I can see her gaze reflected. I stand behind her to see what she is seeing and in all these reflections all that is offered is Zafon's mirror of "what we already carry inside us, that when we read, we do it with all our heart and mind…" (*The Shadow of the Wind*). And with all reflections there is also the troubling notion of refracted light. Maybe I shouldn't have used the prism of hindsight to let the light through, as that way we end up with rainbows everywhere.

Spanish bee Steps

Bumbling along the Alhambra
early morning
black-bodied bee
shines in the yellow iris,
dark armoured
among the startled calendula,
stages a flyover
wing-turns to the cypresses,
from high on the red castle walls
dive bombs the orange blossom,
robbing nectar from the lavender
levels its body among the white
flower flags of peace,
taking off its helmet
hangs its head low
the humble-bee
gets lost in los girasoles,
meanders in the mil flores,
hovering in the myrtle
maze-time siesta,
collects its gold tithes
from the adoring
low-lying poppies,
brings home the holy grail,
and al crepuscolo
dances la bamba
in the ruby faces of roses.

Cocoons and Silk

With time and patience, the mulberry leaf becomes satin.
— Maltbie Davenport Babcock

Down the road from our house were mulberry trees where we sourced food for the silkworms we kept in shoeboxes. The spinning of silkworms' cocoons – now there's a symbol of childhood – spun like threads of toffee, as soft as summer's hum that lingered in the solitude, soothed and enclosed in a world entirely of its own sweet making, not seeking solace, entirely self-contained.

My mother would tease out the silk from the cocoons of silkworms and tie it into soft bows that we pressed between the pages of thick books such as *Blinkie Bill,* the quintessential Aussie tale of a koala full of both bleary-eyed innocence and gumption. Or in the *Magic Pudding* book that would make my brother laugh out loud – much to my mother's delight – as he read it over and over to himself, absorbed in the moment of fantasy and fairytale.

In the secluded space of her own garden my mother would sit so still while the wrens with their brown miniature bodies would strut and flit and flirt. Their primitive scratching claws cling, their beaks bob to and fro, on the look-out, their all-seeing rusty-rimmed eyes see and accept. And it sounds like a conversation: "I have this to say" and "What do you think?" In the pause there is silence, complete silence and then the indecipherable rejoinder. And their feathers as soft as no sound, cushioned on the still air.

And in that silence I imagine my mother gazing inward and further inward, to the perfumed, petalled centre of a rose; it takes her there to hushed words, in the drift of the day. Like the silk that has its beginning as a worm, like the cicada and its beating song, like the bee and its honey, nature reveals the terrestrial and celestial in one.

A Bee in the Moment

Watch me forage
in the unfurled face
of the sweet briar –
in the furrows of its smoothed brow
her purpose to blossom and flower,
the two of us in unison,
unmitigated mission,
our communion unswayed by drafts of scented air
resonate in reverence, botanic prayer
like meditative om, the sirens' sea-soft song,
intent in the moment, lingering long.

Bliss, Bees and Butterflies

To make a prairie it takes a clover and one bee… and revery…

— Emily Dickinson

Learning to wonder, that's a life lesson from my mother … and from all my favourite poets. Not hard to do if one really breathes in nature's joys; their truth revealed, they give life a bigger meaning. It's like turning a leaf over and spotting some hidden bug or the brown on the shining underside of a magnolia leaf. The wonder of nature and perhaps a sense of creation itself, however, did not mean for my mother a "need to go to church to kiss silver plates … For one can know him as well in a wood, in a field, or even contemplating the eternal vault like the ancients" (Flaubert). Church hymns rather than birdsong were to her ears tuneless. And certainly, with another sort of reverence one can know a mother's vigilance. It's like the wind moving across the undulating silken wheat fields, parting and smoothing.

Peonies in profusion
Perfumed by brown-furred bees
And papillons ripple-winged,
On polished pomegranate cheeks.

Snoozing and The Hum of Bees

Can't resist the intoxication
Complete
In timeless contemplation.
Intensity and lethargy
The richness and the rarity
The massed abundant blossom
The humming synergy
Silence forcing to the horizon,
The wings beating energy,
The gentle iris blue.
Soothing warmth
Lures to surrender
To dozing dreams.

Resting on succulent leaves, butterfly wings vibrate the air, rippling its reminiscences from one garden to another from back then and now. And the little child reaches like a mantis praying to catch what is not ours to catch, just to know it, to grasp the wonder of it.

In a blissfully unaware existence, a child's typical afternoon might go like this, a microcosm of innocence and being in the moment. It probably should be told in the David Attenborough tone used for documenting the life of a particular species:

> He wakes ruddy-cheeked emerging with
> a tussle from the afternoon nap. Cautiously he
> peers and senses for signs of safety and

benevolence.

Smiling in recognition of the resumed schedule he is as full of gumption as a gecko, clicking and grinning. He begins his fearless, stocky toddling, robust and speedy, a battery man. The bounces of the blue ball bring a certain self-satisfaction. His pincer fingers pick up tiny scraps of paper in dogged retrieval. In the sunny courtyard he looks overhead for aeroplanes and listens to birdcalls. Sitting in the laundry-basket eating a peanut butter sandwich – doesn't get much better than this – he smiles and chomps, this is all that has to get done right now. He looks to our faces, his compass for response – should I like this? Is this OK? He nuzzles into a velvet shirt and chews it just to know it and take it all in. Next he climbs the stairs and clambers backwards. Over and over. Then with some self-moderation he takes to just hanging – lying on the step, gazing at the ceiling.

During the four o'clock passeggiata in the stroller, he reacquaints himself with his neighbourhood whereabouts; he is distracted by children at play, cars parked, helicopters and magpies – and with his finger, like a conductor's baton, he keeps the rhythm of the afternoon proceedings. When he arrives back at the gate, another smile shows his delight in returning home.

A determined, marching crawl to the pantry indicates a Pooh-Bear interest in a "little something" – though that empty muesli box is pretty distracting. At dinner, tasty morsels intrigue him with textures and flavours. No mistaking when his taste buds are offended, but mostly he eagerly receives in his open bird-like mouth all that is on offer. He also takes a spoon filled with yoghurt and attempts to feed himself.

Now it's time for an after-dinner bop. Who's being entertained here? Time to change gear in preparation for a peaceful bedtime – he looks at a book and puts the sticky-tape roll in the Tupperware container, again and again. He rubs his eyes, he has run out of puff.

Now he becomes king of the bathtub. He splashes in his playground. Holding his toothbrush like a wand, he is towel-tousled and moisturised. All glowing and calm he is lullabied into a night-long sleep.

For my mother, Louis Armstrong's song about this "wonderful world", with all the enchantment of the innocent, as we watch them grow, chimed well. It is like a toddler's smiling delight in peeling a banana, completely being in the present moment without even knowing it. That same presence is like the grandmother's vigil or the mother's kiss on the head with that fulsome, wholesome "I love you" kiss through which she draws you into protection, both hers and the child's.

That was my mother's gift to me – she allowed my childhood to be happy. It seems I had the existence of the quintessential child. We rode bicycles in the middle of the road and snuck up on cicadas. We were as giddy as catherine wheels, more vibrant than sparklers and as alive as Tom thumbs. These thoughts are throwbacks to the times of throw-downs, explosives in miniature, pyrotechnic thrills. There was no artifice, we were as awake and brave as the orchestra of fireworks at a burning bonfire night with the brilliant smiles of the firefly. And dazzled in the cold dark we crunched on the sweetness of meringues in our mittened hands. No sense of excess or envy, no gluttony, no guilt.

Bananas and Butterflies

A moment in a boy's beautiful day,
see the grateful smile,
in the filtered light,
a yellow banana, lucky delight
he takes care
to reveal its edible form
remarkable in its disguise
he discovers anew its surprise;
ears tuned to passing sounds
a small voice mutter, blue eyes peeled,
follow the wing flutter
the spotted black butterfly
that chanced to come by
into the drift and space of his garden.

Humming and Hydrangeas

Let parents bequeath to their children not riches, but the spirit of reverence.

— Plato

Fat slugs with horned heads hung out in the jasmine that grew over the roof of the outside toilet, and hydrangeas or hortensias grew against the garage. They didn't seem to hold much oratory for me, they were just sticks through winter and in summer they would reliably bloom blue in neat rows. A far greater distraction was to watch the bees dancing on points, humming and bouncing off the sharp petalled tips clustered into the whole floppy flowerhead with a single stitch.

Each Christmas-time, my mother would wrap a large bunch in ribboned cellophane for me to take to Mrs Openshaw, an elderly lady with white hair in a bun, who lived a few houses up the street, and who greeted me with sweets and smiles. That was how, for years after leaving home, I tended to think of hydrangeas, not really appreciating the solid abundance of their bloom. But back then I would simply hum through the hours in harmony with the waking and closing of each day.

The Hortense has no pretense
round, substantial and bold,
dependable, pink or blue?
whatever suits you
when you're old.

Backyard or Beyond – rhus trees and rhubarb

Come away, O human child: To the waters and the wild
with a fairy, hand in hand,
For the world's more full of weeping than you can
understand.

— William Butler Yeats

In November when the toothbrush blossoms appeared, you would see us climbing high, fearless, into the branches of the giant silky oak tree, a grevillea robusta. Sunlight streams in sideways through the silk-shiny leaves and the flower spiders burnished like an eagle orange eye under a furrowed bark brow, as we keep watch on our backyard.

On many days at that hour, just before everyone came indoors for the evening meal, a sound often heard in our backyard was the back-and-forth hollow ping of the shuttling of feathered corks hitting wooden-handled bats as we played shuttlecock with my mother, when she wasn't keeping watch over pots on the stove. It was a game that taught us an agility and coordination that never really went away. One particular time when my grandmother visited, her hair thick like my mother's and mostly in a grey soft chignon, she taught me to catch a ball in the backyard. Even now when I catch a ball it brings me back to her, and to my brothers playing French cricket. Her intense black-lashed Irish eyes seemed to see much more than we did.

On the surface of the backyard pool like a wide-open sea, with his own Robinson Crusoe spirit – a castaway, facing the storms, and letting the wind fill the sails – my brother used to launch his toy sailboat. It floated and tossed and battered against the sides until he righted the keel and restored its balance. It was a sandstone pool built by my father, a weekend self-taught handyman. There we were all brought up as water babies and would swim every day for the sheer joy of it. And so did my mother, well into her later years.

Whether down in the river, or in Sydney Harbour, or our backyard pool, in our underwater scene the sounds were muffled, our feet were off the ground – we were suspended in time and space and spirit. We were like Tom who fell into a river and turned from a chimney sweep into a water baby in an underwater magical world, like Charles Kingsley's *The Water-Babies. A Fairy Tale for a Land-Baby.* Captivating children and parents world-wide, the story was recreated as a movie in the seventies, with the star James Mason. We were ignorant of the subplots about poverty in industrial England, a century before, something loomed below our naïveté. That, however, is the privilege of childhood, not to know. How strange it still is to learn late that so many things were happening in the world outside of our own – the salt of sorrowful tears, the sense of injustice in children's eyes, the anguish on a mother's brow in time of loss – while we filled our days with splashing and laughing; the worst that might happen was little more than to tread on a bee in the clover, lose a favourite marble, or scrape a knee.

So as the Child is the Man

He steers his shoulders gently
into her embrace
as if not to admit too much;
he melts into her touch
on his very soft cheek;
he purrs in tune
with her rhythm
fingered on the veins of his temples
as if to stay in that time forever
suspended out of the reach of any harm.

Childhood and cats' paws smell like brown – rich, of the earth, secure. I remember the cat rolling in the dirt and licking its fur for hours, and letting me take it for a stroll in the pram, dressed not as the fabled Puss-in-Boots, but as my own baby doll. Our family always had a cat, one called Blackie because it was, its sister Stripey because it was, and one called Woolly because it was.

I see our cat stretching and curling in a sun trap on the patio of our double brick home, a Californian bungalow in a suburb in Sydney. There we would spend sunny hours playing in cubby houses, make-believe whispering hideaways and secret clubs, set with scaled-down chairs and tables and teacups, in a Lilliputian world, hiding in tunnels made of cardboard cartons, and shunning the light at the end. And we literally hopped, skipped and jumped our afternoon away, chalking our squares on the outdoor paving, and negotiating with purpose-made stone or lead taws in our daily games of hopscotch – a preoccupation that only matters in and of itself.

But now I'm jumping through memories with a grasshopper mentality, leaping in and out of childhood close-up shots. Grasshoppers – backyard leaping grass-green springboks of our quarter acre block. Bug-eyed and stalk-horned. Escaping capture, their spring-heeled spirit never to be contained, they were thriving.

Also thriving, were the dark oversized oxalic leaves of enormous bunches of perennial and steadfast rhubarb, expanding in the mulched soil of the back garden against the paling fence. The rhubarb, ruby and rampant, was hacked down with a sharp blade and the bitter stalks were transformed for the family every week into teeth-catching sweet nourishment.

In our front yard was a fine-leafed Japanese maple with autumn colours that matched the red of the rhus tree leaves that my father would religiously rake up fearing that we would all end up with allergies. The prongs of the rake reverberated with a twang on each stroke across the grass beside the bed of lavender with its thin long spikes like indigo soldiers, steadfast, marching to the sound of chores of a Saturday afternoon.

A thousand ants

black march across the soil
they upstage the dance of cicadas
by their smug relentless toil.

Fair and Foul Play

Fair is foul and foul is fair
Hover through the fog and filthy air.

— *Macbeth*, Shakespeare

The lessons of the backyard taught us a sense of fun, fair go and fair play, though not necessarily competitiveness, nor a killer spirit. Training in sport was more about just honing one's skills to be better and better but there was the thrill of the sport which took precedence over competitive angst. Imagine my mother as a teenager and school champion, free-spiriting across hurdles as she did – jumping hurdles was something at which she learned to excel.

But we, like much of Australia, had not yet grown up nor yet had arrived at the luxury of dedication to sport. Still, proud we all were when Dawn Fraser had such swimming success and when tennis greats like Rod Laver led the world. And proud we were when we ourselves won family swimming relays at sports carnivals. Both my brothers grew up surfing and one ran marathons – were they both chasing the thrill of success or simply pursuing something that would take them out of themselves, engrossed in something where they could truly be in the free spirit moment? Like when our backyard was the site of kayak-building. Perhaps the boys imagined themselves setting out on Thor Heyerdahl's *Kon-Tiki* expedition, journeying across the Pacific Ocean, exploring an archipelago and seeking out welcoming sandy cays, guided by an Inca sun-god's benevolence, keeping them safe, for now.

On one particular weekend, as a Brownie raising "willing shilling" charity money, I was asked to pick up piles of rhus tree leaves from the yard of a neighbour up the street. With bare fingers and a rusty rake missing a few prongs I took earnestly to shifting decayed autumn leaves, in dense stacks rusting into the dirt and matted grass. My fervour was repaid with extreme allergic rashes on my skin that took months to clear. I don't think my mother ever forgave that neighbour, with his own form of backyard bullying.

Foul and fair were interchangeable in some witch-like minds. My mother recalled that in her own yard, as a child, she saw the result of terrible cruelty the day her family had left their beloved dog, called Bob, playing with a bone on the lawn. When they came back home they found it had been kicked to death. It was a harsh lesson of her childhood from which my own was comparatively sheltered.

Dangers lurking for us were more about snakes beneath the snare of blackberry bushes as we picked off the prize of precious blackberries. Or perhaps the undertow beneath the waves that was a threat but not a hindrance to the thrill of our chase of the surf. No, it would be a long time before our outlooks changed and we came to realise that all is not always as it seems. And to see that in life's games both foul and fair, most of the time we're playing in a fog that might clear to show us things we never wanted to find out.

Blackberry Monologue

Blackberry canes
hoisted on the wind
dry and rasping
on the sandy slopes
of muted melancholy
by the silent sea.

Black ruby jewels
bezelled on the bushes
dazzled with the glaring light
they fail to thrive, then shrivel,
impenetrable briar patch
entangled in its cross-hatch.

Pale empty eyes
screwed up tight
against the lashes of the wind,
searching, she peers out across the waves,
her tongue tastes the salt,
she squints and on her brow there's a frown
and here on the sand she starts to drown.

Pea-shelling in the afternoon

Better to lose count while naming your blessings than to lose your blessings to counting your troubles.
— Maltbie Davenport Babcock

Childhood memory sits me on the back step as the sun goes down behind the towering silky-oak tree where my brothers and I had been climbing earlier in the day. The black and white currawong calls from the high branches. And I sit and shell peas and count them for our dinner thinking of sugared pancakes spread with butter and lemon. Then the lemon-rind sun dips into the grainy background of the melted butter sky. It's the pea-shelling ritual – calm, quiet, productive, as I pay attention to the green wonder of nature's packaging. There's something about the naive smell of raw peas.

As the afternoon light faded on the pea-shelling scene I would step back inside, and my mother in her ironed apron would be standing at the kitchen bench – a formica top in the 1960s pea-green. Framed by the open doorway she would be standing with her outline in front of the window, crossed with timber bars. As if on a movie set, signs of a meaning beyond the banal were there, only we weren't looking. With dedicated ritual, my mother prepared dinner. Typically, it consisted of meat and three vegetables – usually including minted peas – then our spirits were plumped with pancakes or pudding that was self-saucing. All placed in front of us, and eaten without comment or question.

To the left of the kitchen sink was the revered Mixmaster appliance, an object with a split-pea personality, channelling serious and dedicated pursuit of pleasure and nourishment. With this wonder of household progress my mother would churn the mixture for a butter cake or beat the egg whites and sugar for the meringue topping of velvet pudding, raspberry jam-lined and custard-filled. And we would lick the blades of the beaters clean.

To the right of the ordered kitchen bench was the sink with a strainer to prevent a clogged drain and a rack for letting the dishes dry without wetting the ironed tea towels. In the cupboards below the sink there was an economy-sized tin of chocolate Aktavite, absolutely guaranteeing vitamins and minerals suitable for growing children's health. In the corner there was a round metal cake tin with the word *Cake* written in italics and biscuit tins stocked with biscuits we had bought in a brown paper bag down at the local general store. Tea, flour and sugar canisters in matching pea-green were there in a row on the shelf and for quick access, over there on the bench stood the metallic squat teapot with its tea-cosy, plain-and-purl troubles and blessings knitted in multi-coloured woollen rows, and a slight tea stain turned to the wall.

Butterfly Cakes

On the tip of the creamed butter
fly's shivering wings
she pulses her intent
reverberating soft-spoken air
all around our cheeks
until we tremble
with her tremors.

My mother's precision in measuring and mixing ingredients successfully produced so many of our childhood favourites – the cookies that melted our moments, the pudding that was our bread and butter, and the stewed apples. Her thanks and her pleasure were our keenness of consumption. The sugared froth from the stewing Granny Smith apples rose up from the pot on the stove and the steam wafted its warm goodness through the rooms of the house. Our nostrils filled with the cloves and cinnamon scent cutting through the apple sweetness. And we drank the warm juice just poured from the pot into a glass, pure appleness.

Lemon-squeezing and Lighting Candles

We open the halves of a miracle, so the freshness lives on in a lemon in the sweet-smelling house of the rind.

— Pablo Neruda

My grandmother's home smelt of lemons, another one of those scents that disguises nothing, it just is, we inhale its unmistakable citric freshness. We would drive to their home in the beach suburb of Avalon many, many Sundays. Being a dutiful son, my father would mow their lawns, determined and as ruthless as a leaf-cutter ant. My mother brought her twice-blessed baking, once for its nourishment and once for its selflessness.

My grandfather would treat me to pencils and blank exercise books with lined pages where I would work through the mental arithmetic problems out of the books that he had written for school children. Meanwhile with her benevolent smile, my grandmother served us homemade chocolate hedgehog biscuits and lemon tea. Grandma's slow squeezing of the lemon was part of the tea-making ritual over the course of the day. It gave some sense of progression across the hours filled with little else in an elderly person's day. The child, on the other hand, has little sense of time as every minute is filled with the preoccupation of make-believe and play and someone else orders the day's passing – from the sunrise cup of tea until sunset arrives again.

But lemons also draw me back to our neighbours in my childhood. My mother had befriended the charming Austrian lady, Maria, next door, who lived there as a single mother with her son and a boarder in a spare room. And a German Shepherd dog called Catullus. Maria had seen war from another angle so distant from the Australian experience, and with different tragedies. In her clinging to the well-lit side of life she fascinated us with lighting real candles on her Christmas tree – real pine like ours except ours was garlanded with coloured lights in all different wonderful shapes like glass pinecones, candy sticks and fragile long-tailed birds which my mother had chosen and which each year would blow a fuse, sending my father with his own short fuse into a spin furiously trying to fix them. We were used to my mother's own labour-intensive and skilful baking, more our everyday experience, but Maria's cakes were truly out of the ordinary. She would invite me in to have tea parties with my dolls and best manners. We would sit on chairs beside the Christmas tree with its candles all alight and classical music records playing with that background crackling somehow reassuring and part of the wonder of it all. It was a fairytale world of indulgence. Such a special time always – that leap of joy like a fat raisin squelching with buttered glee, drunk on liquid laughter.

Red-faced bauble – you shine and turn
your cheeks start to burn
catch the glint from a child's giggle
a thousand fairy-lights jiggle.

School Days – milk, marbles and Mercurochrome

…it is the business of the eye to make coloured forms out of what is essentially shimmering. This is how we "get around" in the world.

— Rachel Carson

In another childhood moment I hear the sounds of unchecked giggling at school play lunch and still see the bubbles of milk blowing out of our nostrils. Until it's time to sober up for the next times-table race, the next spelling bee and story-writing before the final bell sounds the child's spent day.

All had been going well on my first school day through the sitting on mats for singing, through the painting, through the writing in new lined exercise books, through telling the time with the wooden moveable clock hands, through the play-lunch of dried apricots and nuts. But then came lunch when we had time to wander farther through the playground. It was vast. The largest school playground in Sydney with long stretches of grass and sticky paspalum weeds, garden beds around the flagpole, basketball courts and dirt patches where older children set up stumps for cricket. And suddenly in all of that I had no idea how to get back to my classroom. Tears welled up, so alone with so many children all around, but no familiar face or place. Then when my brother Graham saw me he took me by the hand, and back to my classroom, telling me, "It's OK Bub."

After that day I embraced all that school had to offer, only I never managed to master neat writing nor avoid constant ink blots on my middle finger which still bears the writing bump, like a student's rite of passage. Nor was there much success with embroidering hucker-back hand towels, nor sewing muumuu dresses – that was so much a part of my mother's talent, for me just a neatness challenge. It was as if in all the hours my mother mended with needle and thread she fabricated for us a flannel-like blanket, warm, it seamed us in. But it was woven with silk fibrils we could stretch and unravel and reshape.

A challenge that held more fun was marbles. My brothers had huge hordes of marbles of all sorts and all the playground lingo to go with the game – Tom bowlers, the oversized marbles, cat's eyes, aggies, made from agate stone, oilies which were opaque with a rainbow finish, steelies, multi-coloured swirlies. These were carefully guarded and on the way home from school they clacked and clunked and clinked around in primitive triumph in the red draw-string bag that my mother made and that I still safe-keep.

Every Saturday morning, I was off to another form of schooling which aimed to instil a sense of goodwill, practical life skills and the fanciful world of the Brownies. And with a gumption and eagerness to dance around imaginary toadstools, learn knots and maps and follow stepping stones to reach the fairy pond – a mirror set among leaves and petals arranged in the make-believe woods where fantasy grew like dandelions and creatures kept watch with their soft coats like the pet cat's but ever so much softer. The weekly routine for some time also included, yet again, scraping the same knee with the encrusted scab which my mother would mercurochrome against bacteria. As if that was all it would take to shield one's children forever.

Mind's eye

Close your eyes.
A child again.
They can't see you.

Ritual and Routine – tea and truth

Drink your tea slowly and reverently as if it is the axis on which the earth revolves – slowly, evenly, without rushing toward the future. Live the actual moment. Only this moment is life.

— Thich Nhat Hanh

These unfolding snippets of stories hold whimsical truths and nostalgia for times now gone. Perhaps the words might make tears drop into your teacup like Alice's tears in her Wonderland, not to flooding proportions just that welling up that comes when a heartstring is tugged, a memory of your own jolted, a chord strummed, another time and place recalled. As in Alice's world, telling a story gives a doorway that magnifies our life or makes it small to fit into the frame.

Tea parties with miniature China blue cups are a typical recollection that would fit into the small frame of our day by day. The usual companions at this tea-making were dolls with their own names and assorted home-sewn wardrobes, as well as a fair-furred bear with brown corduroy trousers and a button eye. And China was a place that produced Oolong tea which came in a luxury hamper of treats from faraway places all round the world and landing on our front porch as sent by my mother's uncle from Melbourne.

My mother would take her tea with milk and daydreams, and sometimes flick through the made-up stories on the pages of women's magazines. Or she would read the willow pattern story on the china saucer, watching the lovers cross the bridge into an eternity. It was always a calm process – she had adopted the attitude of being deliberate, considered and unhurried in the process. Perhaps in this way she found Blake's eternity in an hour, in the scrawls of the hours of each day with its own punctuation of commas and dashes, giving her pause for breath and contemplation.

But then onto the bed of nasturtiums she would throw out the wishful tealeaves that failed again to have anything remarkable or any certainty in their forecasts except for the likelihood of day following night. Gypsy fortune-telling had some lure for my mother, though always a fear as well. This stemmed from a time when as a girl she had opened the door of her home to find a gypsy woman standing on the doorstep. She stared at my mother and said to her that she would have a very sad life. When her mother arrived at the door she shooed the woman away. She actually said "shoo", as though the woman were a fly. My grandmother was of course protecting my mother and probably was a little superstitious about the ominous words. In fact, my grandmother's deep and nervous mistrust transferred to that gypsy figure a fraudulent authority, crediting her with clairvoyance, even though she was just a spinner of tales. And left standing on the doorstep was my mother as the child with a rag doll dangling at her side, a willing believer. She then went back inside to drink her morning glassful of milk truth at the kitchen table.

After disposing of the tealeaves in the garden my mother, as the adult, in her own home always returned to the task at hand whether it was with a rolling pin or a washing line or a meat mincer.

That was a Monday afternoon ritual for me, to mince the leftovers from the lamb roast, squelching the chopped pieces of lamb and onion through the metal mincer secured to the kitchen bench. That meant we could have Shepherd's Pie, topped with mashed potato for dinner. And so our daily routines were regulated by our family dinner menus or our menus by our daily routines.

At this moment

Those leaves are so green
they seem to leap
outside of themselves
with joy;
the breeze turns in the glare,
green-fingered jabs
dissect the light,
intense benevolence;
born just now
new-nubbed bursts
force our gaze
to now and near.

We used to see swallows in the eaves of our school classroom verandah. They are said to be the harbingers of change, symbolising uncertainty as they flit in different directions. It seemed that swallows were everywhere but we were not attuned to their signalling.

My mother's life was lived by rules and routines – but they went so out of fashion. We do grow, however, to see their place, their importance in regulating potential chaos, whether through a baby's lack of sleep or an adult's faded fitness. Her days revolved around her family's needs, and in a myriad of ways I recall the things that were proof of this, even in a small way, as when she made a blue velvet case for my recorder, or sewed my dresses, darned our socks, put our clothes in front of the heater in winter before we dressed, made us a hot breakfast before school, heard our times tables and vocabulary lists, made a nutritious hot meal and dessert every single day after the loads of washing and ironing and on and on with the rituals of a purposeful day lived for others. In family life my mother was indeed "completely present" as in the philosophy of Lao Tzu.

Something my parents might have forgotten to do in later years was to "Look up at the stars", as the late scientist Stephen Hawking urged. While my mother encouraged us as children to look at the night skies, in solitude did she gaze any longer into the deep blue, the colour of somewhere she wasn't, beyond lists and schedules, routines and measures? I wonder really how much any of that was a part of her own existence where there was not the luxury of time nor indulgence to seek something beyond daily duty. If you are used to following a pattern that you use for cutting out fabric to make into a garment what do you do when someone tears up the pattern? What do you do when those rows of knitting are unravelled and knotted?

Home and Hearth

...living together in the small things and the day is bound together in a dear domesticity...

— Stoneback, 2010

Recollections here are being reconstituted like the green cordial of our childhood or raspberry jelly prepared for the trifle that was more than a mere trifle. Its festive purpose was to celebrate, to make things larger than life ... to take us outside of ourselves. So many moments like that I still recall.

My mother's greatest sense of place was the love of their home. She decorated and gardened and cleaned with pride and gratitude for what they had. My father similarly filled his weekends with mending and building and barbecuing. Simple pleasures were their way of life. In a small way I am reminded of the characters in the movie *The Castle*, because of their satisfaction with their lot, so that they could also have used the famous line, "How's the serenity?" They had built their own sandcastle, only fluorescent lit and built in fact on Sydney sandstone. For my mother, home was where one starts and ends.

Out from the kitchen there was a long sunroom warm as cat's fur in winter and a place to play on rainy days. The decor was nautical-themed with glass-ball fishing floats criss-crossed with jute netting, together with banana wicker chairs and clam shells from the sea voyages of our neighbour, a ship's engineer, and on the wooden shelves there were contorted pieces of driftwood collected on long beach walks, all giving that weary-worn insouciance.

Sometimes in the sunroom, in our earlier childhood, my mother and father would sing while he played the ukulele and we would dance to 1920 songs such as *Yes Sir, That's My Baby* and *Bye Bye Blackbird*.

Later when my older brother needed to study, the room was divided, and the decor replaced with a not-sure-what sort of seventies look, with new brown bean-bags, chrome ornaments and orange mushroom cloud lamp. The other end of the sunroom was divided off to make a separate space for my brother with a bed, a desk, his guitar and a collection of shells. It seems to me that each shell was a home for an unseen and unknown memory. The creature recluse had recused itself from having to attest to the meaning of life and had gone elsewhere. Besides what does it matter now – the creature has had its redundancy highlighted by a light bulb placed in the hole drilled through the side of the conch shell.

On the wall of our living room were paintings of Albert Namatjira, with their subdued colours denying the shrieking harshness of the land and conveying a sense of another world where dreams were dreamt in purples and ochres. Like the gas flames in our fireplace. Next to it were the home-made timber bookshelves where Eleanor Dark's *Timeless Land,* written in 1941, held much more than indigenous dreamtime and landscapes and much more than we understood at the time.

There also in the living room in front of the television we would ride on horseback with Annie Oakley, thrill to the vine-swinging moves of Tarzan and jump over quick sand, and side and chant with the Indians – brave and braided… all from the comfort of our stream-lined, modern and dust-free couch with its rhus-tree red bouclé woollen covers. Beside the couch was a nest of coffee tables useful for balancing the evening cups of tea. And the ceiling fan oscillated with the sounds of family life – alternating activity and serenity – lifted into the air, a draft on our brows, reverberating from then to now.

Through the antique-painted bi-fold doors of the living room there was the dining room where all our meals were eaten in a quiet, restrained way with the correct use of cutlery. With my brothers I would sit very upright, with my feet not quite touching the floor, in upholstered chairs at an oak table with a beaded timber edge. Napkins would be rolled up at the end of the meal, threaded into engraved silver napkin rings and put into the heavy drawers of the oak sideboard.

Off the dining room was my room. My mother had hand-painted a timber dressing table and chest of drawers in optimistic turquoise. The wall against the single bed was where I turned to in my sleep for its cool touch and the reassuring closing off from anything else. Inevitably I would get one leg stuck between the bed and the wall, as only a child would do. On the wall were small china plates painted with the artwork of an indigenous painter – one showed a beautiful little round-cheeked girl with dark curly long hair dressed in a ballet tutu and pink satin slippers with ribbons which trailed at random, enticing me to go dancing too, though my mother thought that after my first successful year perhaps ballet was for more precocious children and their mothers. With some choices in life, feet should really be kept on the ground and the head out of the clouds.

Outside my bedroom window closed off with venetian blinds, in the early morning before the rest of the household woke, I would lie in bed and stay tuned to the endless cooing of a dove. I can see the hand-made stone block wall at the edge of the garden, the rouged ranunculus and the anemones persuasive in their purple black-stamened statement, in their stance unsure of what has been or will return. The wisteria leaves drape across the gate with its rusty-edged lock and I can wander with my eyes to the secluded garden beyond, a hideaway from voices, the paling fence a dove-grey disguise of storied memories. All the while I trace out with my eyes the pattern of the cornice moulding at my bedroom ceiling, over and over. How often did that dove coo? It was an untimed repetition, a long meek chiming of the timelessness of childhood.

Bug-eared Poet

Sitting on the step, antennae out
Alone but keen
To communicate.
Your footsteps loud on the staircase
Vibrate a message
Compounding the others
I collect, collate and crunch,
Masticate morsels of material
A synthesiser of raw sounds
Useful to the cause of messaging,
And transform it to my own song.

SPOTLIGHT ON HEATHER: HERITAGE, HISTORY AND HOPES

I will not look at the gold of the evening which falls,
Nor the faraway sails descending towards Harfleur.
And when I arrive, I will put on your tomb
A green bouquet of holly and flowering heather.

— Victor Hugo

Sandpipers pecking in the sand on life's shore, that was our family life. We did manage sometimes to fly away though only across oceans of fantasy. But now we turn to pipers of another kind. Scottish traditions and bagpipes – a strong part of my mother's upbringing as Heather Henderson. Her Celtic background through her Irish grandmother and her Scottish grandfather who travelled to Australia, as well as some European heritage, gave her a sense of the romantic, beyond the everyday.

Certainly, the story of the Huguenots captured the imaginations of my mother and her younger sister, Lesley and brother, Eric. It seems that our ancestors in the eighteenth century – perhaps silk-weavers or booksellers or nobles – between edicts of religious tolerance escaped from France.

Imagine the thrill and sense of risk in the story of a woman hidden with only a flask of water and a couple of loaves of bread inside an empty wine barrel, ready to be stowed on board a sailing ship heading for Britain. At any time a soldier might by chance halt a rumbling barrel on the dock and slice into it with his sword to check if it were wine or an escapee while the hidden Huguenot would ever so quietly hold her breath, not safe until far out on the open dark sea.

According to the family legend, her ancestors were famous for their strength, and certainly that was a quality that my mother would need over a life of many testing times.

She was born a twin and her grandmother fed her whey with an eyedropper nurturing her to survival but her little brother did not survive his first few days. There was possibly an unsaid commitment for my mother to be a survivor from them on, full of determination. Her early childhood was full of warmth from the secure care of her grandparents in their Melbourne home, while her parents travelled back and forth to Sydney for work commitments. She would be chauffeur-driven to and from school, roll pastry out with the Scottish maid, Nettie, and keenly collect citrus fruits from the long backyard orchard.

Proud also was my mother of her Scottish name, Heather – the flower of the moors, a thing of gentle beauty and of free spirit having to withstand great harshness of conditions and endure. But for now she is hearing the bagpipes with their reservoir of Scottish air blasting their ancestral message on the woodwind, the haunting notes push through her veins and she flings her highland steps across the distant moors.

Sandpiping

I need to go over there to see me
Over that line between sky and sea
I long ago touched down on the sand
Don't leave me forever to stare and idly stand
On this shore so secure
But with chances fewer and fewer
I could stay here forever and a day
But I need simply to cast away.

Inventions and Inventiveness

To us, the value of a work lies in its newness: the invention of new forms, or a novel combination of old forms, the discovery of unknown worlds or the exploration of unfamiliar areas in worlds already discovered – revelations, surprises.

— Octavio Paz

In a Model T Ford sit my mother's Irish grandmother Elizabeth Stenhouse and her Scottish grandfather James Kerr Henderson with their first born, my mother's father, William Stenhouse Henderson. In the photo that I keep on my bookshelf I can see the family in their car and in its undercarriage are the springs provided by Henderson's industries, the family company that competed in international progress and breakthroughs. Their city depot was established in Elizabeth Street, Sydney in 1920s and Elizabeth Ralston Henderson founded the Henderson Industries company, the spring industry of Australia. My mother often told the tale of being among the very first people to cross the Harbour Bridge because of her family's contribution to its building including the bolts in the steel girders. She was proud of her father's achievements as an engineer, of his inventive spirit, perseverance and ingenuity. That, together with happenstance, in the true spirit of innovation, brought new possibilities.

Creative sparks were part of the family thinking and so it was that my mother's father was forever inventing and building things in new ways. With the caravan that he had designed and built – perhaps a pretence at living a gypsy existence – her family went on holidays to remote Sussex Inlet on the south coast when my mother was 13. As it happened my father, only 14 years old at the time, was also holidaying there with his school. He had the ingenuity to offer to carry water for my mother and that was the beginning of their very long relationship. They wrote letters, he from his family home in Maroubra, "on the other side of the Bridge" and she from hers in Roseville, on the north shore of Sydney Harbour. A couple of years later they met up after his parents moved to Lane Cove, on the same side of the bridge. He wrote one time in a letter that he wanted to marry her – a big thought for a young man, he said. It paid off to have big thoughts. And she kept forever in a brown leather wallet the cut-out snippet of the letter.

He wrote that letter from the country town of Glen Davis. No-one knew where it was exactly, an oil shale mining town with a small population, far out in the country but that's where my father went at the age of 17 after he finished his education at a selective high school. He was sent there as a bank teller. It meant he could earn an income and relieve his parents from paying for board and university tuition. While he was there he wrote to my mother. With not much to do in a small and remote country town, apart from football with the local team, he carved a heart out of shale and put it on a wooden block as a gift to her – perfectly his style and it seduced her imagination with its earnest simplicity. She kept that heart for the rest of her ninety-two years.

Red — Roses and Blood

The bloom on its straight stem
Red fragrance
Too fragile to touch,
But red prized petals
Its thorns defend.

She turned crimson.
Red is excruciating discomfort
It's the colour of cheeks
Bare with red shame
Inadequate, insecure,

Red raw.
Red is unveiled passion
Revealed rage and desire
Fury and fire,
Roused emotions.

She salves her burning skin
Red with irritation
Pared back skin
Scraped mercurochrome knees
Coagulated crusts.

The russet leaf falls from an overhead branch
Red in the filtered light,
Right in front of her,
It falls at her faltering feet
To signal time is passing.

Across the fading skies
Red is the sun downing
Its sorrow below horizons
Out of sight
Blind now to bright light.

Out on the field the poppy
Red draped on the grave
Of the boy whose blood
Spilled at the hands of just another boy
As he too lay dying.
Red ... enough now is said.

War and Wisdom, Smoke and Mirrors

Pack up the moon and dismantle the sun.

— W.H. Auden

If we were to look closely at my parents' sepia photograph taken in later wartime years, we would notice my mother's movie-star beauty and her dramatic gown of delustred satin, with thirty covered buttons down the bodice and intricate lace across the pin-tucked shoulders. But we should look again at her eyes – soft with sadness, bloodshot from tears, as my father was soon to go back to war. It was December 1944. In that year she had turned twenty-one. My father recorded in his much later years that "she was all any man could ever want".

There were many war ghosts in my mother's stories. So often she would return to those stories of the charm of soldiers she met, their kindness and sometimes their self-assured, urbane ways, silk smooth. But of course it would take more than a pair of silk stockings to turn her head, it was just a facade, just a surface glimmer and glamour with no depth. War itself, they say, was a theatre, perhaps it made soldiers larger than life. And at the time it was as if it gave some purpose, some certainty like suspenders that hold up stockings, not the stay-up kind that don't. As part of keeping up appearances, in war-time Sydney, women drew lines on the backs of their legs to pretend they were the seams of stockings which were scarce and which they couldn't afford. The silk stockings that American soldiers visiting Sydney brought to impress their potential sweethearts stood for fine luxury, a smokescreen, you could hold up a mirror on a snatched sense of fun. Meanwhile there were many real ghosts, however, that continued to haunt the nightmares of my mother and father long after the war.

Wearing her pretend stockings, suit and hat, my mother would travel on the bus to the city to work as a bank clerk or as a telephonist. On the bus to work she had taken to reading the dictionary to expand her vocabulary and simply because she enjoyed words. Perhaps they were something that made solid sense. Perhaps in some ways she lived through reading. I'm imagining that on the bus she looks up from her page and turns to stare out the window with words and thoughts of war woven in her mind. Out there, people are fast passing in gloves and anonymity, hat brims pulled low over searching eyes and coat collars upturned, complete and closed in on themselves. Can we hear the whispers in the street of a woman who might pass us by? Enveloped in ordinary circumstances, what do any of us know of others' pain, doubts, insecurities, of their strength, drive or the source of their inner joy. As we jostle along we might bump the elbow of someone's mother who lived for her family and had always been steadfast in that purpose now gone. Then my mother returns to her pages as if she could fill herself up with words and so possess a knowledge that would be her shield and her way to keep growing in a war-driven world; to be her own protagonist on an antagonistic set.

Also touched by the drama of war and a sense of inevitability, was the marriage story of my father's parents. It began when my grandfather returned from World War I which he had rushed to from university years, with the flush of anticipation, lying about his age. After fighting in France, he recuperated from injuries in a hospital in England. There he had a crush on a nurse but as if theatricality had to be put aside he returned home to Sydney to marry his real sweetheart, Dorothy Christabel. I loved those names, both down-to-earth and fairy-luring, at the same time though, I don't recall noticing many fairies in their backyard.

In all this memory sifting, one looks for a sense of destiny and for omens or life's signs. But perhaps this is a matter of chasing illusions. Instead we keep to the here and now like the shorebirds. The philosopher Frankl suggested that "we create what we choose to be" and so a life lived is a life chosen. It would still make sense though to keep an eye out for what might be beyond the shore… just in case. So we watch for the first signs of stars in a delustred satin sky. And we seek to make sense of glimmers everywhere.

Doors Opening and Closing

…we often look so long and so regretfully upon the closed door that we do not see the one which has opened for us.
— Alexander Graham Bell

New opportunity and excitement, that's what the flying moves of the "dancing man" signified in Sydney at the end of World War II. The image captured the hearts and minds of Australians who went dancing in the streets with relief from war and with new hope. There he was with his hat outstretched and with a gracious bow, greeting joy itself. Isn't joy what we all want to know and keep close forever? No wonder my mother returned so often to recounting those moments when war had ended. She was there that day in George Street in Sydney, August 15, 1945. The leaps of elation were broadcast on a black and white movie newsreel, with the radio-star voice of Jack Davey putting peace on a pedestal.

In the years after the war and through the births and raising of three children, it was as if my mother and my father had made a pact to get on with life but only to concern themselves with the here and now. That meant bricks and mortar, food, hard work, schools nearby and a secure job. Secure and purposeful like picture frames. None of those rustic, borer-ridden timber frames taken from old doors with too much nostalgia – tidy it away, make things new and shined up again. That sentiment at the time was probably not uncommon, not wanting to go too far away from the familiar, to make things normal again. Hankerings after what else there might be were tamed, no time for illusions, time to get on with real life, making a safe harbour. Besides, as Thoreau pointed out, "fools stand on their island opportunities and look toward another land".

Stopover at The Pigeon House

On the road again, passing through,
Just want a home, can I rest a while?
And feel safely home, secure as a pigeon.

So the family of sandpipers now would peck at the sand and the grit, they would stay grounded as it were, no need to fly to other places or look for what was beyond their means or anywhere beyond. Nor even a need to imagine, even to consider the allure of an arched doorway, framed with intricate mosaics from faraway places, inviting nomads to enter – do we dare go through?

And some doors just stayed shut. My mother had indeed regretted missing the opportunity to travel to Switzerland to go to finishing school where young women went to finish off raw edges with the smoothing iron of etiquette and protocol and propriety but much more than that, of course, they went for the chance to meet others across the world, exploring other possibilities. The outbreak of war had finished that. She had enjoyed the responsibility and the camaraderie of working in the bank but it was her default option as she had always wanted to go to university to become a teacher. The door had closed.

A questing personality which I have come to

recognise might be a privilege of our times, would have wanted to prise that door ajar. In my mother's time, however, household duties so often tended to fall mainly to the women and fully preoccupied them. As regularly and routinely as folding and unfolding the laundered bed sheets, these soft drapes of memories make us wonder. But their world was filled with red lipstick optimism and hope, always my mother seemed to navigate between those two emotions.

Lull

I wait for it –
that hushed watch of the water bird
its speckled feathers smooth,
that stillness of the lithe cat
lean limbs stretched at rest;
that halted breath
held in the semi-breve;
that filled hiatus
at the very end of long-drawn breathing,
that rush of froth and trouble
stilled to silent pause;
that quiet in your being here,
that gap between the furrows on your brow.

Fashion and Frivolity

Fashion fades, only style remains the same.

— Coco Chanel

On outings to town to go shopping or see a movie, my mother would wear gloves and a hat, moderately high heels and seamed stockings, a grey skirt and blazer with a pearl brooch and white silk blouse. Over her wrist she commonly wore a small black leather handbag with a simple gold clasp that snapped shut with a decisive end-of-the-matter sort of clunk. When the handbag was opened the fragrance of the satin lining filled the air with its notes of tuberose. There she kept her coin purse, comb and lipstick – always red as my father preferred that – and always a lace handkerchief, an artefact for heartfelt hankering. In the side pocket she would put the bus tickets, for safekeeping in case the inspector arrived on the bus to check.

Other times we might catch the ferry from Circular Quay to Manly for a big day out with milkshakes and sandwiches cut in quarters. On the ferry we would notice how the ferryman, with the skill of a sorcerer, flicked the slithering rope, shiny sleek in his handling of it, around and over, backwards and downwards in easy loops over the silver crucifix until he held us tight to the shore. Not yet time to venture out. And then the quick piping of the ferry's horn and we would rush away on a new adventure in the sunshine.

My mother's casual fashion commonly included capri-style zipped cotton pants with short-sleeved shirts in summer and in winter she wore woollen skirts checked in scotch blue, not unlike her Henderson tartan, and round-necked pullovers. Other times she wore dresses with wide belts and cinched in waistlines – though my father was sceptical of dieting, after the scarcity of good food during the Great Depression and then rationing during the war, why would we want to deprive ourselves of good food?

Besides, he thought my mother's face would become too gaunt. And skirt fabrics could billow like sails now that fashion had moved past the austerity of leaner times. Corsets, however, helped to regulate and overcome a fear of stray plumpness.

But what of bikinis and miniskirts? Seemingly at odds with all that. And burnt-orange dresses, Bermuda shorts and baby-doll dresses, all of which we might have seen on the television show *Bandstand*, tuned into every Saturday night. All of these my mother was happy for me to wear – she might indeed have been a dedicated follower of fashion.

First and foremost, my mother felt she was a wife, mother and housewife – very much playing that role of that era, some degree of independence and interest, however, came through her part-time work. She was delighted to work at June Dally Watkins' modelling agency in the 1960s. That was a way to be in touch with glamour, the beautiful as if real and the unreal. Perhaps it was a chance for her to show the more outgoing and playful side of her personality.

And so, in all these musings on life, we feel in our fingers the common threads of lives lived then and there. While a writer might take these threads of ideas and weave words, the real seamstress was my mother. She rejoiced in fine quality fabrics – silks and satins, mohair and bouclé threads, linen and organza and cotton *broderie anglaise* – far from the days of the roughness of boiled wool, like soldiers' uniforms. And I remember that she liked to shadow-stitch delicate fabrics, hiding from clear view yet revealing what lay hidden below, like the murky waters among the mangrove swamps. Every season she would create a new outfit for me, and for my father and the boys – the knitted vests, the darned socks, the reworked collars, the patches, the seam adjustments, the turning up of cuffs, mending the rips and tears of the lived out days.

Silk and Scents and Sea sirens

Hustle rustle with the tulle of tutu
Crystals, pearls galore,
Gaudy gems and bursting bijoux,
She's selling seashells by the seashore,
Entrancing frills and fine frou-frou
Spider crabs dance on a seaweed floor.

Squinting at our days through sequin prisms-
Uncurtained light, our dazzled sight
Wide, gaping, shimmering schisms-
After the dulled long-waking night
See teeming fish in glinting precision
Waters warmed by soft-sung daylight
Plunge deep in sea-scented indecision
On wings in cloudless seas take flight.

Landscape and Lustre

Tels sont les paysages, échos de l'interminable dialogue entre l'être et le faire, entre l'homme quit veut marquer et la terre qui de sa peau n'offre que la surface. (This is the essence of landscapes: they are the echoes of the never-ending dialogue between being and doing; between people who want to leave their mark and the earth, which offers them only the topmost layer of its skin.)
— Erik Orsenna of Charles Cartier Bresson

Fibro cottages and sometimes tents, always without glamour, these were our family holidays. Humble and down-to-earth, they never failed to allow us a real glimpse into the wonder of the changing light, the saturated rose and violet, bleeding into the water-coloured horizon.

At the change from summer haze to autumn's copper-coloured chills, we would take a long drive out over the Blue Mountains to Oberon at Easter time. On an enormous sheep farming country property, with its lichen-covered rocks, and breezes through the gums and pines, we set up camp so that we could go trout fishing in the dam. Our faces were reddened by the sun in the heat of the day and by the campfire at night when the temperature dropped to zero degrees. We braced for the intensity of temperature extremes of each day. With it there was a spirituality of place, a rustling of uncertainties through the dry grasses and the oil-soaked leaves of the towering gums.

At morning light over the water, low cloud would hover and fill my line of sight with its fine particles imparting their poetry, binding into an impenetrable meaning, one replicated from the teased out white silk of clouds in wide-blue skies stretching from yesterday. The sun's morning light filtered through the mist slinking along the hills, and fractured on the crunch of frost at the edges of the dam, flickering on pointy icicles that fingered our lines. We cast and trolled the spinners to lure the trout with false promise but when least expected one spinner would drop from the line, a dead weight, never to be retrieved, sinking into the mud.

Dragonfly

Prism of rainbows
Iridescent in the shadows
Dipping low to the water.

In a frenzy of camp-building we would place newspaper sheets under the stretcher beds to keep out the chilling moisture. On a small rise of land my father would set up an elaborately constructed hole-in-the-ground toilet complete with a seat almost like a throne surrounded by a hessian curtain resplendent. And unfortunately transparent against the western sun. Outside our tent there was a bucket of water for washing but it froze over during the night. We could see snow on the other hills but where we were it was just freezing.

And I can see in that scene the dapple-barked birch standing steadfast in white, and the poplars majestic in the freeze of the land. The willow is weeping with melting frost. The mist leans to the land like a silk throw, its translucent threads stretched across our gaze. The cherry tree branches push out nubs of ice blossoms. Low to the ground below moss-crusted tree trunks sequinned grass tussocks pull up their blankets and the grass matting is criss-crossed in sage ice. Not for my mother all this harshness of the elements nor the cartel of carping crows that collected like hunchbacked omens over the sheep carcasses and pecked through her sense of tranquility. After a couple of trips she stayed at home, probably blissfully enjoying some serenity though this never occurred to us as children totally in the moment of camp life, fishing and bonfires. One time we laughed to see a lamb follow my brother for about half an hour until he jumped onto a rock in the dam. And just like the nursery rhyme lamb that followed Mary, our lamb just stayed and waited for him. And meanwhile with our patient fishing, mine was the only trout caught by the only girl in the camp – which made my mother smirk with pride.

Most times when we would go to Oberon we went with another family. They were Catholic, a fact only relevant because it meant they would go to church mass on the Sunday morning early before we "heathens" were up and about. On their way back, they would buy Easter eggs for us, a pagan reward.

Even then I noticed the fury that my father would go into as he packed the boot so that everything was in its place and every possible contingency of strife was covered with his usual foresight and efficiency. The other family, in contrast, threw everything in the boot of their spacious station wagon where nothing had a specific place. Nor did the father seem at all interested in making it tidy.

As it happened, his brother was the writer Nino Culotta, author of *They're a Weird Mob*, a politically incorrect yet sympathetic portrayal of Italian migrants so numerous at the time, who had come to assist with the famous Snowy Mountain Scheme which involved, simply put, major dam-building to help generate hydroelectricity, a project that children learned about in school social studies and today is much talked about as a source of energy and renewed political interest. The migrants became so much a part of Australian way of life. In our family, racism was a naive attempt at wanting to make sense of the Europeans' foreignness, relatively unaware that we were foreign to them. When we saw big Italian extended family picnics at the beach, it struck us as strange, because we did not do the same, nor sample the same opulent menus, but it would never occur to any of us not to befriend or assist. There was a certain naïveté of spirit.

Trust

I like poplars.
Their leaves show their underside.

Picnics were in fact a part of that naïveté and a part of life for our own family of five. They created an occasion, humble though it was. My mother would bring cans of pineapple juice tasting of over-ripeness, savoury thirst-starving biscuits with sliced tomatoes, and a home-made butter cake with passionfruit icing, all set out on a blanket at the beach, with plates and cutlery from the picnic set, and a special miniature set of joining salt and pepper shakers. Everything was salted and peppered always, the food more seasoned than our conversation. One time we traipsed the length of Palm Beach with all the paraphernalia for a special lunch with my grandmother and my mother's sister, Lesley, who had made one of her sponge cakes. Much to her chagrin, my brother Graham made the point quite loudly that there was eggshell in his piece of cake. While my mother might say Graham was cheeky, she probably was actually admiring of his spark and his grin. As I remember it, my mother seemed to take some sibling rivalry delight in this eggshell lapse and retold the story a number of times.

Paradise Bird

Long-nailed khaki fingers
slender parted reveal
a space of blue
stirred by gusts
chilled, disrupting
the rolling surface
dash-dash-dash.
And just beyond
an open empty launch
its canopy blue and faded
shading the white bench
where the fisherman
sat early on the tide
and caught the eager

lured and snatched
surprise on the dawn.
For now the sun warms
the orange plant birds
lit up in paradise
outwards searching,
far-seeing to the next shore,
here, intent, the worker weeding
at their heroic feet.
And so begins
the reassuring smile
of a new unfolding day.

Castles and Creeks

There is not a particle of life which does not bear poetry within it.

— Flaubert

Deep and still in the green-dark water, reflections show vines creeping up the trunks in stealth, furling inwards, hanging low. Shadows shade dark trunks, evergreening their way through a silent existence, unmoved. Still broad leaves catch the light that seeps into their mindset and they shine their promise from the moisture in their veins. There in the brackish reflections three children dropped a fishing line out of the windows of our grandfather's boat shed on McCarrs Creek in Church Point, near Sydney's more northern beaches, where we would go from time to time for a weekend's stay.

My mother loved to reminisce about her father pottering around, as yachties do, for the sheer pleasure, engrossed in their own moment, like Ratty in *Wind in the Willows* "simply messing about in boats". My grandfather had happily retired at forty years of age from engineering and spent a lot of time designing and building and sailing boats. The image I have of him is as a stocky man, his knees slightly bent while standing in his old corduroy pants, hair slicked back with light oil, and commonly a benevolent smile on his face that now I know to be debonair, though his lips and mouth reminded me of a dormouse. Often there was a cigarette in his hand. One time when I was about five years old my brothers and I found his cigarette papers and tobacco in a drawer in the boat shed, so we rolled our own.

"A place by the water" – my grandfather's final property on the northern beaches was given the indigenous name *Quindalup*, a nod to his time spent in Western Australia and also to the fact that he had natural springs on his five acres located close to the coastline. The springs, I remember, were considered by the family to be a rich resource in and of themselves, a source of survival of spirit and body. Later, when we inherited the sign, which my mother had been very keen for us to hang onto, we checked the translation but only found *bandicoot* – much less romantic and an odd name to give to a house. So we still haven't hung it on our own house.

Being by the water was always important to my mother and she could gaze at the ocean or at the still water from her home in Longueville. There she had negotiated the purchase of the land, designed and built her own house by the water when she was around the age of fifty, her dream had become real. For certain, as I feel it now, she would have looked out the window and into that blueness of the water breathing it in with her eyes. It's like watching the changing skies. And there the visual sense is overwhelmed – our eyes are open wide to the colours of the crepuscule clouds and it takes us away. Where did we go? Where does anyone go?

Cockatoos and Sapphires

Being Irish, he had an abiding sense of tragedy, which sustained him through temporary periods of joy.

— William Butler Yeats

In the landscape of recollections, a place that stands out is a small village called Grabben Gullen – an indigenous word meaning 'small waters' – which even now has a population of just 253 people, not far from the potato- and wind-farming area of Crookwell in the south-western part of the state of New South Wales. It was a standout weekend, eyes peeled for shiny objects while constantly taking in the beauty of the gully and surrounding poplar trees. We had the good luck to discover sapphires, one of which was an enormous parti sapphire in a soft sea-green, hidden in the gravel and sand of the creek where we fossicked. Shards of light reflected off the sapphire onto my mother's face as she squinted into the sunlight. Like a trophy, the sapphire was faceted and refashioned into an outsized ring, in a setting that my mother chose with a more artistic eye than my father's.

Gems were my father's hobby and my mother would delight in their magic. I can visualise her sitting on a lichen-covered rock where she would feel the glinting roughness of a piece of smoky quartz, still one of my favourite semi-precious gems. Perhaps she would have let her thoughts drift like smoke, its smell swirling into her nostrils. Her fingers might have circled the sharp rocks on the ground next to where she was sitting as if by osmosis she might know their eternal secrets. The horizon was now blurred but on the rock where she was sitting she could have heard the jangling of the coins that had escaped from her pocket and landed on the hard surface. It made her think that maybe she was paying in kind for past regrets – they were the coins of all her nostalgia for a time to which she could never return or a place where she might never arrive.

Our ordered world was sometimes lit with a particular drama, its richness sometimes hidden. It was opaque like a white opal until held up to the light or when the dull opal potch straight from the ground is cut and reveals its surprising sparks. And just like a child's kaleidoscope we can twist to find the colours and forms we like the most, like choosing the multi-coloured lolly from a packet of fruit tingles – the one we said was a mistake or maybe it was a factory worker's joking attempt at creativity.

Parti Sapphire

Like a glint in a desert of dry
Like beckoning out of the corner of her eye
Guiding like a lure
With a gluttony so impure
An obsidian obsession
Hexagon tougher than obsidian
Corundum conundrum
Hardness of nine
Scalpel sharp but now all mine, "my precious".

With the freedom of a hawk, my mother went flying one day over the vast red rock formation known as the Bungle Bungles in outback Australia. To cruise low over the conspicuous round-bodied boulders in a six-seater aeroplane was my mother's idea of life's thrills, a reach towards the divine. She loved the outback and had a sense of awe and of gratitude for its uncommon beauty. And she was fascinated by its craggy low-lidded goannas, likely to be sunning themselves on ancient rust rocks by a pond of steadfast purple waterlilies.

The words of Dorothea McKellar in her poem about the *Sunburnt Country* rang true for my mother, with its *far horizons* and *jewel-sea*, both beautiful and full of terror, she thought such descriptions with their inherent patriotism were, for her, just right.

That poem sang in tune with my mother's own sense of place and patriotism. It was like walking through the gate of an abandoned homestead of the early1800s with a rusted iron roof, its grey in sympathy with the bark bareness of the trees whose limbs cried out to be massaged with oils to make them alive and blithe. Step over the sandstone threshold and you would find a sloping table, its pinewood smoothed down by the labour of a carpenter – his rusted pliers, spanners, screwdrivers aligned in readiness for a use that would never happen now. It had become the worn-out home of a hermit. His piercing eyes could look straight through you and out to the dust of the plains. His face with a truculent stare is crinkled like corrugated iron and speckled like the wood ducks in the yard with their rusty-feathered stripes. There is a congruity in all of this and perhaps that was what my mother was seeking.

Highlands

And over there
black pointed rooftops
behind long-standing gums,
roadside lichen-covered trunks,
steadfast skyward;
the green undulates
and surprises white goats,
their horns at the ready
and beards tapered;
brown clods waiting for crops,
and right in front of us
the lyrebird turned roadrunner
flings herself
across the highland scrub.

Up and down the coast my parents would go with their possessions in the car boot, once again immaculately packed with spares of everything and muesli. On their many road trips – the closest they would have come to leading any sort of gypsy life through the countryside – they came across characters of all sorts and were interested to hear their tales. Sometimes theirs were tall tales and my mother would say that they had kissed the blarney stone as they danced an exaggerated criss-crossed footwork through their storytelling which aimed to dazzle in a double-cross of untruth for the traveller. But mostly theirs was just a benign wink and nod as if to bring you into some secret.

One of those characters would be like the old whisky drinker, Jack, perched at a bar in dusty Portland where nothing much had happened since the closing of the cement works, as though the whole town had sort of been cemented over and any signs of real life were set in concrete for good:

> Jack's knuckles wrapped tight around the whisky glass were crumpled and creased and dried out. His other hand fidgeted with the thick lines of the fabric in his old brown cords that he wore each night up at the pub in winter with his faded blue flannelette shirt that he'd had for thirty odd years. His face was swarthy from the harsh, cold winds and his eyes creased permanently against the glare and the dust with just pinpoints of sapphire blue. Strands of faded-out sandy hair lay flattened against his scalp. His forehead had dry, deep lines as though furrowed from the burden of not knowing where his life was going or even where it had been. What had happened to those years since the war? How had he filled their every day other than labouring at the cement works along with most men in the town. What else had he thought to do? Who else did he need to know? No sailing over any ocean. What else was there beyond the horizon over the parched hills except the next dust-filled town where you might want a few extra supplies every now and then? Out there the cockatoos made you stop and wonder sometimes. Where did they go

when they weren't screeching at the other birds and ripping off the leaves of the mulberry bushes growing over the outhouse. A person can hardly hear anything over their shrieking. They fill up the sky with their noise – "annoying buggers really", Jack would have said. But better than those miner birds, wherever they come from. They get into everything and steal a man's peace and quiet.

There were plenty of cockatoos screeching in my mother's life. What she needed was to hear the doves coo. What she did hear every day was a caged canary call. There was less sense back then that there's something at odds about keeping creatures of flight caged. My brother kept a large aviary which he and my father built out of chicken wire and timber struts. It was a solid construction, typical of all their diligent work, a spacious habitat for striped zebra finches and a couple of whistling canaries of lemon-butter yellow with a prima donna attitude – each week when the cage was cleaned out they would fly frantically around the cage, chirp a quick ditty and then faint.

What would reach to my mother's heart, however, was sitting out in an open space in the countryside and there catching the day's finch call. Picture the scene – slopes shining with olive trees, dotted with black-ripe fruit, and nearby cows are softly chewing cud, glancing to notice the outline of a human form in their sight, a scene where there is no pretence. It just is. There is an absence of sophistication, no exclusivity – even the neighbour's

Labrador dogs stay close by their masters and the hoped-for food. How fitting that these particular dogs on the farm failed their tests to be sniffer dogs in airport customs. In contrast we see the opportunism of the rosellas snitching at food but of course it is a question of survival rather than malice. Strange that forty years later I would be admiring yellow poplars again and picking olives on a farm not far from Grabben Gullen.

> *Cockatoo screeching,*
> *its irreverent preaching,*
> *holds forth from on high*
> *against a glaring blue sky.*

The Olive Harvest

The olive pickers' day begins;
Three freezing degrees, leaves turn in the waking breeze.
Bent backs merge, melt with the sun rays,
Finchcall shy alerts –
Man with curt secateurs
Invades the boughs.
In the olive grove
The gloved cirque de soleil star
Toetips the branches;
Olive picker chatter rhymes with the clatter
Every olive slipping into the bin
Brimful.
Afternoon grey light
Overhangs silvered olive trees;
The blush of skies now faded
Along with the wearying limbs
Clouds edge the horizon
White as though snow-filled
But the dusk gold glows
On the rim of faraway.

Sanskrit and Sails

What are the clouds like? … I think they are like those purple sails on the golden ship in which Cleopatra sailed to meet Antony.

— Turgenev

Like the crinkles in my father's fair hair, time puts wrinkles and ripples in past images set in small frames. When my father's parents embarked on world cruising in the 1960s they threw streamers from behind the railings as they went sailing away from the antipodes to no idea where. And they sent postcards which we saved and would take out from time to time to savour, in particular the one showing the sails of the feluccas on the Nile, a purple blushed sunset with silhouetted pyramids behind, a world other than ours. It was a trigger for the imaginations of those left on the shore. Revealed in the light on its sails was a mission secret and solitary intended but unknown.

Safe Travels

Streamers off starboard, soon set to sail,
Hear the sighing in the traveller's tale,
Over the horizon, leave no traces,
Crooning of fabled and far-flung places
Rock on the far-watched rising swell
Collecting fictions so easy to tell
The drowning cries of the lone sea singer,
In cavernous shadows the stories still linger.

Our grandfather's letters to my brother John seem to confirm a recognition that life's poetry is, in part, what "travelling abroad" means. Real life is somewhere else (La vraie vie est ailleurs), as Rimbaud told us. We're looking for that "ailleurs", looking for what's beyond our own horizons and yet actually recording the moment with accuracy is evasive. In fact, one day in Columbo in 1962 my grandfather recorded that "the day was very humid and the light hazy for the camera ... Land has been in sight on the starboard giving the owners of binoculars bought in Aden a chance to demonstrate the efficiency of their bargains".

On the idea of capturing images as a precise moment in time as well as their meaning through a particular configuration, the photographer Cartier-Bresson pointed out that:

> To take a photograph is to hold one's breath when all faculties converge in the face of fleeing reality... It is putting one's head, one's eye and one's heart on the same axis. It is a way of life.

For Cartier-Bresson the camera was "a sketch book, an instrument of intuition and spontaneity," and a source of joy that stemmed from a particular perception in an instant. Perhaps the photograph is a poem of light.

A more solid example of a photographic recording was Grandfather's black and white postcard of an elephant in Katugastota in Kandy. The postcard as it happens, was printed in England. On the same voyage my grandfather wrote from his ship, the S.S. Strathmore, that just as on a movie set, the ship kept sounding its siren in the mists. Grandfather's words, written near Gibraltar, captured some of the looked-for drama of the voyage:

> We are experiencing very dense fogs and the siren is sounding continuously; a few hours later another ship loomed up out of the fog and almost rammed us to the intense excitement of all the onlookers.

He finished his letter with grandfatherly advice to my brother reminding him of the "fleeting nature of youth," as though perhaps he was a character in Joseph Conrad's novel of the same name.

Outflier

Lone,
sea-salt solitude
suspended
against the wind
kite-spinning
winging sails
dipping flight,
freewheeling.

Perhaps it was the start of my curiosity to know more about what lay beyond and a wanderlust that would never go away. Staying on the shore or setting sail, things happen that make us change tack but what do we make of that? The need to put "one's head, one's eye and one's heart on the same axis". And that's what made the trinkets from their travels so alluring yet so much a part of that era – hand-carved ivory figures, jade elephants, the inscrutable soapstone Buddha figure, the silver of filigree bracelets catching the light. Postcards have their own artistry and it is after all, as Kandinsky pointed out, the artist's hand that causes "vibrations in the soul".

Is that what piqued the appetite for travelling beyond the horizon? Looking for the dream island in the 1958 song, *Santa Catalina*, the island of romance, with its tropical trees and serene sea breezes? I'm imagining my father sending a message to my mother who would revel in being taken away on his simple and humble sea-sung poem to their own Santa Catalina:

If I had to I would row across the seas,
Sails set to harness the coolness of the breeze
Floating cross the miles and miles,
To see your mouth broaden into knowing smiles –
You knew I would be there – how could I not?
I had to be there just in case you forgot;
I would face the frenzy of the rush of foam,
Guided by albatross flight, steady I'd roam
Keep gazing to the sky, you'll see our same moon,
Froth in a frenzy, flying spume,

Squelched white on the wide canvas of the sea,
To your arms now I need to flee;
Can't see how anything else has mattered,
The breaking glass triangles of waves shattered
My heart as though run aground
If you weren't there in my horizon newfound
Through the salt sands my message might sift,
Leaving me alone there, forever adrift.

Music and Musings and Movie stars

The dance is all there is.

— T.S. Eliot

I could call my father a practical crooner – a mixture of the gentle romance of the tenor voice and self-taught musicality. My parents often sang Eddie Cantor's jazz blues song, *Makin' Whoopee*. They would be dancing away and singing to the tongue-in-cheek story about the conflict between responsibilities and fun, as I see it now that was the same as pecking at grit like the shorebird or flying away.

My mother's background in music was more classical and formal than my father's. At boarding-school she was strictly instructed on the piano and practised devotedly so that she became very accomplished but in fact it led to nothing. I like to think that my mother should have been playing Tchaikovsky on a celesta, making those sugar-plum fairies fill up the room with grace and light. She chose instead to listen with my father to the popular songs of the day. They together sang *Ain't She Sweet?* and *I'm Gonna Wash That Man Right Outa My Hair* from the movie *South Pacific*. Was each song another one of life's sleights of hand that tricks us into believing that this is all there is? When she had to let her piano go because her mother asked for it back she never again played. Eventually she had an electronic keyboard which she soon after gave up because of the pain in her arthritic fingers. The music room in her mind became soundproofed. She maintained, however, a love of music but rarely listened later to classical music.

But then again there are other glimmers in memories of my mother's love of music that make me think of her admiration for Spanish flamenco dancing, fulminant and fabulous with its frantic foot stepping. She loved the gypsy dazzled colours of polka-dot swirling skirts in the frazzle-taggled riot of movement.

The cinema was another form of entertainment where my mother was willingly taken away to a fantasy world. Movie-making meant blinding audiences to realities, embracing stories played out on an outsized screen, with the grandness of the music. And the roar of a full-maned lion makes us all listen up to the tale that will unfold and we become engrossed in the stars' luminous performances. My mother, like all movie-goers, was then free to unashamedly and unapologetically live alongside the movie stars, to weep and laugh and stamp her foot with the petulance of Scarlett O'Hara – played by Vivien Leigh; to admire Humphrey Bogart's valour, and feel the resolve of Katherine Hepburn or the courage of Ingrid Bergman; to succumb to Gregory Peck's charm or be seduced by Cary Grant's cool sophistication, and to thrill to the wink of screenplay heroes blurred behind the vaselined lens. And there was the glamorous Sophia Loren who wore flouncy skirts over her voluptuous bella figura, and Audrey Hepburn, vivacious and elegant, in 1961 wearing her little black dress with pearls in abundance and a pillbox hat in *Breakfast at Tiffany's*.

Film stars were part of a new life that was in fact larger than life. Perhaps my mother, like other movie-goers was looking to the star makers for inspiration while trying to make her own in miniature. Just like a star herself, a photograph of my mother might show her in dreamy soft focus as if in a fairytale film, her arms stretched at ease out from her body in contemplative pose, her wrists and sheer silky summer robes draped across her knees, sepia skinned, curled thick brown hair smoothed with the trick of silk over her hairbrush and shining with a haze of light on individual strands, her toes bare and lightly resting in the sand.

Strike the Pose

Take up positions for the next snapshot
Find a luminous face in the make-up pot.
Delete the frizz with bristle hairbrush
You know it's not real, it's just all airbrush
Snapshot in broad daylight with pretense she demurs
And instead they smudge it into dusk's soft blurs.

Melodies and Makin' Whoopee

Human speech is like a cracked kettle on which we tap crude rhythms for bears to dance to, while we long to make music that will melt the stars.

— Gustave Flaubert

As I write I am thinking that the synergy of a whole piece of music is also a question of the notes one chooses not to play, as the jazz musician Miles Davis said of his music. Omissions can also reveal, they are part of the meaning. And I would never be able to include all that could be included from the tunes of my mother's life, but simply retell what I can hear. What does the child really know, when a mother wraps herself in songs like Nat King Cole's *Mona Lisa,* where *many dreams have been brought to your doorstep*? As if spreading her wings and taking to the sky, just as in the strains of Gershwin's *Summertime*, my mother would float with its dreaminess and soothing lyrics into which she was so ready to be drawn, truly wanting the stars to melt.

Murmurs of bygone melodies fill my listening ears with nostalgic notes in minor chords. The old songs play. The faces and voices of various people and places filed through life moments in my mother's stories. Were they might-have-beens, could-have-beens? The sense of what if, when a road is not taken? Her own road was here, and now and it was impossible to see beyond. Imagination played that role so what better way than to immerse ourselves in the fantasy and rhythm of songs and of stories, though not our own, listening to sounds that bring a new expanded way of seeing life. Sometimes I wonder, did her inner metronome pause while she synchronised with the tempo of family life.

Dance with me

Twirl me to the moon
Caress the notes on soft air
Croon me a smooth tune
Sing out the rhymes on the stair
Dream with me and swoon
Call out loud that we don't care
But don't stop too soon.

A voice is something that can take us away on its lilting waves. My mother would often comment on a particular person's speaking voice and intonation. The movie stars Richard Burton and James Mason thrilled her with their voices, always she was susceptible to the melody of a rich deep voice that seemed to strum her memory chords. Listening to the lyrics of Nat King Cole's *Nature Boy*, I can hear exactly the tune of a wished-for life in the lilting harmonies as the "enchanted boy … shy and sad of eye" wanders far. And I find I am also lilting in a dance trance across those seas.

On the score of dancing, I can in my mind's eye see my mother and father flirting with the beat of dance songs and with each other as they move totally together around the dance floor. Perhaps that previous joy at the declaration of peace was re-conjured when they danced again together. And the dancing man might be just behind them doffing his hat to their joy. Perhaps they had turned into Ginger Rogers and Fred Astaire as they foxy-trotted across the wide floor. Yet even in visualising that or looking at an old photograph which captured the moment, I am recalling the *Cicada and the Ant* fable from La Fontaine, a part of my childhood and theirs. We know that the ant was prudent and worked to stock up for winter; the cicada on the other hand danced away his summer which left him unprepared. The ant, his neighbour, refused to help him out. My mother was surely negotiating their lives between the two – she never chose the way of the irresponsible nor asked another to help but she would relish the chance for dancing, while she could.

Dance of the Innocent

I was swirling a twirling
Dervishing circle of dizziness.
Smiling and gurgling
And unended.
On nothing depended,
But inner motion.

Posies, Peonies and Poppies

A bee staggers out of the peony.

— Matsuo Basho

This simple but powerful image evokes the point in time when a pollen-drunk bee emerges from its suspended moment among the heady perfumed petals. My mother would have loved that sketch. That exacting moment captured like the still life of the flower arrangement, a synthesis melded to the importance of the whole. Like day-by-day life, it is designed, constructed and arranged. Composition was ordered, in particular in Japanese flower arrangements which she also loved. Perhaps they represented something exotic but in most arrangements there were rules according to correct proportion – each stem, for example, had to reach three quarters of the space above the level of the vase. It was about regulation and constriction – like posies for example – which were tight, patterned combinations of a variety of small flowers. It was my mother's precise and perfumed posies, beautifully crafted and ribboned, that gave me an opportunity to present one and curtsy to Queen Sirikit of Thailand at a Brownie and Girl Guide meet in 1962 – an occasion with ceremony and a sense of the exotic and so much excitement that we could almost lose ourselves in the posy's tight spiral of miniature concentric circles.

The scarlet and starched garb of the japonica blossom, a growing still life in the garden each spring, provided material for her flower-arranging which she taught to others. Every spring and autumn surprised us with bulbs that were sprouting jonquils and snowdrops and crocuses. Along the side path, many, many Icelandic multi-coloured, multi-nuanced poppies grew, their petals and hairy stems leaning in disarray but organised in serried rows recently hoed, their startling yellow song in chorus with the purple salvia against the brick wall.

There were poppies too, never the Flanders red poppy and its melancholy, though she loved that in combination with wheat and cornflowers, their blue her mother's favourite; or love-in-the-mist, a pale star with tendrils infinite in their whimsy. And a child could listen out, ever so silently, for the pop of a poppy's petals pulled back from the tiny dots of the yellow stamen, a pincushion for a bee. And appreciating the dancing pink and white of the ballerina fuchsias is a memory her granddaughters will always have of their Grandma. A haven for a child wandering along the side path humming and looking out for signs in the starflowers. Or for those "pisser" cicadas – so-called for obvious reasons – that my brothers and I found up in the branches of the silky oak tree.

Perfume and Petals

They'd take you away
like the flowers of love-in-the-mist
in a traveller's tryst
with the soft-speaking grasses
of a winter's walk along a laneway.

My mother would probably agree with William Blake that heaven could be seen in a wildflower. Her knowledge of plants was vast, as was my older brother's, also focusing on Latin botanical names. Down in the bush where my brothers and I played for long afternoons, we felt a spirit of place imbued through the wildflowers like the spider flower and heath. And the wattle blossom balls that attached to the fur coat of our black cat as it rolled in the dirt in our garden. And the cotoneaster tree's red berries that we used as harmless missiles. Even now, with her toddling great grandson's pincer grip, he innocently enjoys taking a "ball" from a vine of green pearls for his plaything.

But back then, out of my mother's window, the fennel had gone wild like youth's dreams before they've turned to seed, before they've turned to what might have been; the vine leaves trailing, the jasmine leaning in to the outdoor table and chairs still alive with the chirrups of crickets and children.

Impervious marigold

Petals manifold in damp cluster
More intrigue than bloom and bluster
Ruffle their russet and brazen gold
... and the ant climbs out.

Pearls and Perfumes, Pom-poms and Pomp

Be what you would seem to be – or, if you'd like it put more simply – never imagine yourself not to be otherwise than what it might appear to others that what you were or might have been was not otherwise than what you had been would have appeared to them to be otherwise.
 — The Duchess in *Alice in Wonderland*, Lewis Carroll

In obsessive pursuit, for many years my mother made her pilgrimage to the northern cities of Broome and Darwin in the cold months to soak up the sun, the sunsets and pearls – sometimes from the Paspaley pearling family. There was a romantic side to her interest in pearls as she was fascinated by the stories of the risks that pearlers took on their luggers to satisfy their lust for lustrous sea treasures. Maybe a pearl was her amulet. She pursued her pearl quest when they visited us in Hong Kong. My father went out shopping and ended up with a safari jacket – the fashion back in the day, though I'm relieved to say that he never actually wore it. I think he just had some sort of sense of obligation since the Kowloon shopkeeper had offered him a beer. And a chair. Meanwhile my mother was shopping for an exquisite pearl necklace with an emerald clasp. Hers was a belief in the endurance of something beautiful.

My mother also had faith in the monarchy. She liked, I think, to see some parallels between the life of Queen Elizabeth II and herself – the Queen was just a couple of years younger than my mother and her first born, a son, arrived in the same year as my mother's first born and perhaps, though it is clearer now than then, the Queen in a different more elevated way of course had her own sense of balancing duty and pleasure. Her deportment and fashion sense were exactly as my mother would have perceived they should be. Queen Elizabeth II, modelling a white dress that showed off her tiny waist, the quintessential mark of a beauty of the day, came to visit Australian in 1954 to huge fanfare. In a similar way today, royal weddings and the lives of the royal family continue to ignite interest in something grander and in the pageantry and pomp that they say the British do so well, is acknowledged as a way of making life larger and celebrated. The joy of a fairy tale wedding still excites the people who really want to have faith in something inspiring and joyful, taking us beyond the everyday. And my mother was a true believer.

The Pearlers

They set their lug-sails,
Devil winds take them
Through treacherous storms
To deep waters becalmed;
For the sake of adornment
On perfumed soft skin
Pearls fastened at the lover's nape.

Twinsets and pearls, the norm for many women of the fifties and sixties, was later to represent a certain demographic, a certain attitude. But for now, it was part of the fashion in which women had faith. Later we would hesitate to put on the pearls left by a grandmother because it would represent a certain stance and seem to reveal too much of what one's opinions and outlook on life must be – a notion alien to my mother's cohort and yet so significant in my own and across the generation divide. Perhaps they were like childhood pom-poms made on cardboard circles encased in wool – more turning in circles seemingly not making sense – a tactile foible that filled time, just a vain papier-maché distraction.

Like dreams in a bottle, in her crystal perfume bottle with its ornate pillared stopper, she kept her Bond Street floral perfume with its vanilla and warm citrus sandalwood scent. Or sometimes it was Givenchy of the 1950s, with its Parisian chic created by a designer who lived almost over the same span of years as my mother. The echoes of that fragrance are still here – it was a way of breathing in the exotic without going anywhere.

In all these echoes and ripples our vision can become filmy and images hazy. As in old-fashioned movies they become blurred. The fragments of her life are only being viewed with a soft silk-covered lens, like those used for the old time film stars who like my mother smooth-silked their flyaway strands of hair.

And everywhere I look there are glimmers from the bevelled and bezelled days now gone, from crystals and mirrors and gemstones of faraway times. Like viewing an Escher fish in a bird sky, in distilling the meaning of life's moments, there will inevitably be distortions or even contortions of what was seen and understood and believed. And that is the way of the memoir – or at least its fragments – told on my mother's behalf. Even in doing so I am mindful of not putting too much store in the past except to see how the present is reflected in it and how it illuminates what is important to remember, even if in soft focus.

Roy G. Biv

Raucous crimson,
rampant and clammy,
he wears a citrus smirk
in anticipation,
shimmying across reverent skies
robed in saffron.
Exactly at the blue hour
in the lobelia light
he greets indigo Iris
wrapped in violet velvet,
under the wisteria –
they dip down
in a psychedelic tango.

Quirks, Quality and the Quaint

I look forward to the day when world leaders think like the Melbourne housewife.

— Dame Edna Everidge, Barry Humphries

My mother thought that her own town of Melbourne stood for quality. Most Melbourne people think that, don't they? I have a happy memory of the time when after one of her visits to Melbourne to see her relatives she brought back a pale blue pure merino coat with gold buttons – Melbourne being a much better place than Sydney to buy such things – and then she sewed a lambs-fur collar on for extra style. "Breeding will out," was something my mother would quote her grandmother saying, but which she seemed really to believe. And still I seek out lambs-fur.

Avant-garde in her thinking about diet, my mother attended university lectures in dietetics and was au fait with nutritional qualities of a vast array of foods which explained why in that era she put dried apricots and almonds in my primary school lunch box. And probably why I followed calorie counters in my adolescent years. A not so fond memory was the porridge left until it was cold and which I was supposed to finish, as it was an important family attitude to avoid waste.

Then again, lollies while devoid of nutrition had their own drama. Thinking about them immediately takes us back to childhood which some of us have not yet completely left. Freckles with their hundreds and thousands sprinkled over chocolate discs, pink musk sticks and 1947 Melbourne Wizz Fizz sherbet packets.

A fond memory was the time when my mother returned from Melbourne with childly-sweet sherbet bombs, at that time manufactured by a small family business and wrapped in greaseproof paper. A branch of her own family, Stenhouse, had also been confectioners. How strange in a way to call oneself a confectioner but then it seems maybe we all are in the way we manufacture our own confectionery of beliefs. In the sixpenny deal on Friday afternoons we would seek out the good value lollies like the caramel chocolate cobbers, liquorice bullets, eight a penny. And slate pencil lollies which we licked to a sharp hazardous point, like the one that ended up in the roof of my brother's mouth and in the family scrapbook of reminiscences.

Not So Still Life

Rose cloud clusters
splodged into place
on the page
with pointillist fingers
and a smudged smirk grows,
alive with poppies and party pops
in sync with the dandelion
and its pale puffs.

Entertaining guests was always an occasion and we celebrated, as was the trend, with reverent platters of tinned oysters on cream cheese and Jatz savoury biscuits, as well as cocktail onions, coloured red and green on toothpicks set in a wooden container in the shape of a pig. With these there might be a Pimms cocktail drink or a brandy crusta. I'm reminded of the message on the greeting card that says: "Sadly all her creativity was spent on her hors d'oeuvres". It does now seem as though there was some misplaced effort but fashion and insular vision dictated the day-by-day and these remain strong in our collective memories. And of course become a retro trend.

Funny, the earnestness of party preparation. Funny the innocent conversations you have in families. One of our popular topics as small children, for some reason, was to talk about navels or belly buttons – their size, whether they collected fluff, whether they stuck out or sunk in. Inane banter, always a bit silly. I've since seen a children's theme park named the navel of the world – what does that mean? It's a safe place, it's about our beginnings, and the links to our mother that are severed. Strange that I should be recalling it now when writing about my mother and thinking about what it means to be a mother. And who among us ever would have thought that my mother was successfully stepping along her life trail through the middle of what she might want and what she was required to do?

Except when it came to mangoes. That was something she would just fearlessly and flagrantly fling herself into. As if hoodwinked in some goblin market out of Christina Rossetti's poem, my mother would grin and succumb to the indulgence of white "bloom-down-cheeked" peaches, precious pomegranates, or full fragrant figs and their potent juice would be smeared across her mouth. And she would have known she "should not peep at goblin men" for fear of being lured. But mangoes smelt of somewhere else, like the tropics, and tasted like summer sun. Mangoes should probably be eaten in the bathtub she would say. Unaware of portent or pretence, she would slurp on the smooth sliding flesh. And it slid down her wrists.

Harbour Fairy Wake – epithalamion

Green fairy trips across the dross
full of life and lascivious laughs
like a halo of mezcal glow worms
in her whispery fairy-hair floss;
luscious-lipped in a garish stare
in absinthe haze of shadowed light
she leads astray to drowning depths,
rings of fairy lights in the glare
outline the prow, parting waters,
seas of worried witches
hissing and warning,
madmen in purple calling night's daughters,
surging forwards at the titling stern
a phosphorous pied-piper of bridegrooms
daring to follow, searching nearer and near,
bridal veils trail and in the foam wake return
tangled in seaweeds of underwater tombs
the white tulle of steadfastness,
beneath the silent steps of the bride
murky, oil-slicked Xanadu rooms;
choose the swirling water or raging fire
like the newt have faith blind as eyes of bats
take a wide starboard leap to moving land
and sink into the shallows of desire.

Fences and Faraway

Good fences make good neighbours.

— Robert Frost

Far more than fashion trend, or glitz and glamour, in our household things tended to be valued because they came from *faraway*. Maybe that was why my mother collected teaspoons from distant towns – to hold that faraway near. In our backyard we had giant clam shells before a shabby-chic beach house look was so sought after, simply because it was beautiful and from far away. In fact, shabby was what their lives tried to avoid – fix and mend were the preoccupations of the weekends and day-by-day like hospital-cornered bed-making. But my mother would take notice of a faraway look in someone's eyes, something fey, something sad, some longing or just simply dreamy like one of the three sisters who lived next door, one of my best friends.

The hole in the fence episode is in direct contrast to that as my parents had an ever-practical and efficacious way of dealing with difficult circumstances. Our next door neighbour Yves Close more recently retold the incident when my father cut a hole in the fence:

> So often I look back on those early days. You may remember the beginnings of it, when she sent flowers around to me, via John and Graham, soon after we had moved in. And then there was the Sunday when John (her husband) was away at sea.

I, pregnant with Robyn, had a confrontation with a large knife in the kitchen and was bleeding profusely from a badly sliced finger needing medical attention. Your parents were in the back yard and, with no means of transport, I called to them over the fence for help. That was when your Dad immediately knocked down palings in the fence to get me through the gap and drove me somewhere for the wound to be stitched, while Heather bathed two year old Debby and prepared her for bed. The hole in the fence became a permanent gate which, throughout your years in Hinkler Crescent, was very well used. Many times I have related that story to visitors and friends. It is part of our history.

And part of our psyche – that hole in the fence, almost a secret but not. How much did my mother want the opportunity to go well beyond that fence? To see the world, to do what she wanted to do, but also to raise a family and see them go safely out into their own worlds, only not too far away.

Mental Note to Self

They say the long day closes
But that's not right –
There's a door just slightly ajar
And she slips through as if from afar
To remind me of what I should remember –
Dust the porcelain angel in December.

Ghosts and Angels

Shadows and ghosts go through shut doors.

— Carl Sandberg

The image of an angel. That was my mother's acknowledgement, I believe, of faith – in the unseen, the not understood, intuitive grasp ... It was a joyous thing. Ambrosia and manna from heaven were words she commonly used to describe food she liked. Cherub was her term of endearment for a child. A pure white china angel would be placed each Christmas on the sideboard. All this went hand-in-hand with her early religious instruction from nuns at the convent where she boarded while her parents were relocating from Melbourne to Sydney.

In his poetic contemplations of death, in particular of his own child, Victor Hugo spoke of the smiling angel that carried a sheath of souls. The voices of angels are heard with innocence and with joy. And there has always been that uncertainty that if one forgets to pray for the angels they might "forget to pray for us", as Leonard Cohen wrote in his song *Marianne*. While angels have a benevolence and indeed are all sweetness and light, ghosts, on the other hand, have a more equivocal reputation. While my mother did not dismiss them she preferred, if you had to turn your mind to what else was out there, to think in terms of angels and their echoing voices.

On the subject of angels and ghosts, my mother's story has some overlap with this following vignette which tells of a defunct group of ghost writers, who themselves have now indeed become the ghosts. It tells of the memories that linger and make the ghost of a person's life real. The drift of it is this …

Une ange passe

Hush.
Ghost writers have gathered,
Around the polished wooden table-
no reflections returned,
nothing mirrored,
no shadows,
except our writings-
from other times and other souls.
Perhaps our words still haunt
but will they know words like "thistledown"?
will they know apostrophes and semicolons?
Are they now all grammar ghosts,

The residue of our writing days
full of tales real and imagined,
like the legs of a red wine
slipping down the sides of a glass,
truth and fiction, details matter less,
and memories are hazed and flawed,
now memoir fragments,
just catch the drift.

Outside through the windows
the broad maple trees,
full of exuberant leaves,

their rustling muted,
cathedral spires reaching
for their own stories,
aspiring to full-skied expression
of belief and of self.

The pendulum almost silent,
put your ear to the glass clock-case,
hear the rhythmic, reliable sound,
ghostwriters' reverberating expression;
gleaming light whispers
through dust particles,
like airy communications,
the angel has indeed passed by.

Time takes with it what it chooses and what we fail to choose, what we have not clasped to our souls. But time is wise and offers up renewal – that way new generations will also speak with soft voices in libraries – almost anachronisms – metamorphosed.

Ghosts are not ghosts if remembered. Memories are like creaking ghosts – they need attention, they have important stories to tell. More real than those banksia men from children's stories were the swagmen or swaggies – war ghosts themselves, shell-shocked and penniless, the sundowners who hid out in caves in the bush, with just a few belongings in their swags. They were suspended in time, and I can see one now crossing the suspension bridge, ropes on either side of the wooden higgledy piggledy planks wobbling underfoot, as unsteady as their passing idle days. The planks narrowing away, among the imposing gums, looming in the all-surrounding fog, fretful in its indecision. Suspended part way high above the ground, no turning back, enter into the fog, the limbs and outlined leaves merge. Spending their days in restless searching, they might find some night-time peace with the stars overhead.

> *And ghosts have sighed*
> *a milky breath*
> *across the muslin cloth of sky.*

And I think my mother must have been looking for the angel with a lyre to sing to her, to give her strength and exalt her spirit. Over the years she would often go to St Mary's Cathedral, especially in wartime and sad times. There you can breathe in the scent of the cool marble floors, solid and still.

Catharsis in the Cathedral

Right after the catechism
Cathedralled into silence
Down into the spiritual chasm
Uttering a soulful sigh
That relieves the outward chaos
Escaping the fear of cataclysm
No more the bickerings and bombings
Exchanged now for marble sanctity.

Thyme and Timelessness

Mes étoiles au ciel avaient un doux frou-frou. (My stars in the sky rustled softly.)

— *L'Éternité*, Rimbaud

If I go back in time inside the family kitchen, I see soup warming on the stove – the bubbles cooing their soft promise of vegetables and cracked pepper and melted cheese as well as thyme and parsley from the outside terracotta pots at the back door. To the new generation of her grandchildren – Claire and Nicole, Victoria, James and Alexandra, my mother had a lot she could tell. I notice my daughter whispering in my mother's ear, her hand up to hide the whisper from someone's hearing and my mother giggles to be in on some secret and back in the schoolyard naïveté.

This was the innocence of the child who wraps herself in the window curtain peeping through the white translucent veil of see-through-I see-you secrecy. In those hidden moments of timeless invisibility and trust. In our schoolyards and beyond, however, there can also be the painful affront of the "double-cross" and the cry, "But you promised", because the secret and the promise are sacrosanct. But even children in the playground learn fast that not everyone and not life itself shares the same creed, many promises are broken. My mother, however, had created for her grandchildren, as she had for me, a safe haven. And so it should be for their children whom my mother would have loved to meet. In those enclosed moments my mother was completely present; she would be playfully taking tea and chatting.

In all of this I am aware that these are our own reflections as we shuffle and reshuffle memories represented through souvenirs, mementoes – lucky charms from the past – and as Italo Calvino observes: "Every life is an encyclopaedia, a library, an inventory of objects, a pattern book of styles, in which everything can be constantly remixed and rearranged in every possible fashion."

So a timelessness sets in even while we are living our days in the here and now. My mother's gaze is everywhere. There is an increasingly disconcerting realisation that the child is becoming the mother, as more and more tastes and thoughts are discovered to coincide. This unexpected coinciding of dissimilarities becoming more similar is shown in relief when one of our guests picks up the antique asparagus tongs which my mother had given me. I had recognised them as an unusual thing of beauty. This was not simply for the sheen of the silver with its miniature flowers etched in relief and the perfect curled shape for picking up asparagus spears, nor for the patina, which no matter how much I polished as my mother would have polished them, they continued to reflect the many years they've seen. No, increasingly as I hold these tongs, I realise they were important to my mother and that is why I have them – her aesthetic sense caused her to appreciate them for their functionality and their fine-crafted appeal. And so should I.

I need some thyme

Can you tell me where I'll find it?
In the third aisle on your left hand side.
I went directly to that spot
But I didn't find it
No dark, no light
No sunset, no sunrise
No moon, no sun on the stocked shelves.
There were no stars and no rooster crowed.
How will I find it?
Now and in the future?
Just put one foot in front of the other
And you'll see it passing.
Present tense becomes Future tense
and finally Past tense.

Objects, like talismans, give off their own timelessness. Like paperweights. Is that why my mother collected them? Now I can see something of the ringed tight structuring of the flowers in a posy perfectly preserved under glass. Their function though is to hold things down. What was there that lifted up her gaze, that got her spirits to soar? It had been much more than objects but in later times that was all she had around her as she no longer ventured out among her beloved trees and flowers, nor heard the birdcall. She no longer breathed the night air nor knew first-hand the lustre of the stars but the light would have sung to her heart. Perhaps no longer fearful of infinity itself, she might have had faith in Roethke's words, in "the dying of time in the white light of tomorrow". She maintained her wonder at beauty especially in nature – in the bark of the trees, in the beauty of shade and light on the she-oak leaves, in the folds of a petal, in the fragile infinity of a spider's woven web, in the warmth of the sunshine on her back in winter. When she could not watch the moon in its stages so brief yet so enduring, she would find herself out there by sheer will, and as if inside Montaigne's writings she would be "in a state like that of things above the moon, ever serene".

Fragile infinity

In midnight's sky
spun sugar islands floating,
white cream whispers shuffle
across peppered stars.

Marmalade and Slow Motion

Nobody has found a better way to travel slowly than to walk ... it's not performance that counts but the intensity of the sky, the splendour of the landscape ...

— Frédéric Gros

Actually looking into the sky's intensity, listening and noticing the differing lights, slows down time, makes us aware and in awe of what there is. Like lying on the beach and being lucky enough to hear the silence between the waves. Or surf riding, at exactly that point on the peak of the cerulean wave where there is no turning back – there for the ride – embrace it or go under the deluge, into the washing-machine of the sudsy foam.

The luminous blue hour of dusk between sunset and night – I love to be in that alive moment. It is at that time "when one finally finds oneself in renewed harmony with the world and the light". With his perfume *L'Heure Bleue* (The Blue Hour), Jaques Guerlain was recreating the sense of "the suspended hour". The hour of monochromatic colour that you breathe in like a perfume of light.

Perhaps we enjoy the contemplation of the colour blue, as Goethe has pointed out "not because it advances to us, but because it draws us after it". We gaze into the blue yonder – now there's a word from the past – that idea of faraway, wandering if only with the eyes, drawing in and sending back the blueness of somewhere else.

Which comes to mind first – the scent of salt on beach towels or their colours? The compelling and earthy odour of a camphor laurel wooden bowl or its smooth silken touch? The smell of watermelon or its taste? They meld into the slow art form of reminiscences that linger. It's like taking the trouble, as my mother so often did, to soak the oats on the stove overnight to allow them to draw in the moisture and be turned slowly into plump porridge by the next morning. Gluggy and hot with a skim of skin across the top, brown sugar, a knob of butter and a pinch of salt, just as my great grandmother and her Scottish maid had done.

Ode to Marmalade

Rich rounded oranges
From laden branches in Seville,
Their blessed faraway bounty
Rich as amber amulets
Sweet crafted with care,
Mouthfuls of fortune and prayer.

There were bitter-sweet liqueur-steeped jams, slow-matured from the cumquats picked from the heavy-laden tree out the back door. Just as my mother and her father and his father had relished being able to pick citrus fruit in their orchard and we scrunched up our faces with the tart taste of the slow-grown goodness of grapefruits. And there were slow roasts and sauce made from the garden's pungent mint, and slow rich casseroles that sang from the pots; treacle steamed puddings – things that take time and were not for instant gratification – these were a normal part of our childhood nourishment. Things in slow motion.

So keen we were as children to tell the time on our dandelion clocks plucked from the cricket-filled and sticky grasses of the fields on the way to school. But the dust gets kicked up from the bare patches of dirt on the way, the dust specks get into our eyes, time runs away from us and is unreliable.

Postcards from somewhere else.

I feel the spindrift of the years,
its loosened particles
blown moist on my cheek
hazing my eyes
and into my open hand
the reveried sandman
pours hour-glassed grains
blown off the dunes,
far from here
but near,
and laughs rush in with the high tide,
cries threaten on the undertow,
the sapphire tears
trickling out on the shine of the sea.

In the caesura of the dove's song we wait for time to reveal another message, right now. We stop what we're doing just to listen. Slow time, fixing our attention, maintaining a focus on the here and now, on what is abiding. So back at my window desk, the clouds, reflected in the glass top, rush past with the white haze of the moment but I'm cocooned in a serene place. And still the dove coos.

Dandelion Time

I want in no time to be there
On the wind dispersed
Puff floating to nowhere
Sun-whispered clusters
Burst out everywhere
Sinking silk, hushed to still air.

FADE to GREY

Imagination is the only weapon in the war against reality.
— Cheshire Cat in *Alice in Wonderland,* Lewis Carroll

I have reflected on the sweetness and light that is childhood. Good things, right? But here's the thing: the first one cloys, the second one fades. Without the light, reflections turn to shadows, the shapes less visible now tarry in the low light, waiting to be discovered and to have their say.

I am thinking of the dark words of Nietzsche, "if you gaze for long into an abyss, the abyss will gaze into you". But what about if you gaze for long into the light, will it gaze into you? Will it stay with you? Will it linger under your eyelids or will it fade to the pale of sadness? Or just to faraway? Sometimes the world is just like one of those opaque opals.

During adolescent days it seemed that my thoughts and outlook parted ways with that of my parents – not an unusual occurrence in households across the world. I still remember the time at the dinner table where not a lot of conversation went on but after a few times answering, "I think so", my father tersely asked, "Don't you know anything?" Shocked, I hadn't thought my simple phrase was controversial. Clearly for my father it was a very annoying habit that I had, seeing he was more keen on absolutes than on things coloured in the nuances of grey – though ironically he actually liked to wear the colour grey. I remember my mother saying, "I wouldn't ever paint the walls grey ... too depressing." But in fact, it was our thinking that was being painted grey.

There lay the beginnings of an understanding that I had come to think differently and indeed had thought it a good thing not to be too certain of anything, a point reinforced in an early lecture at university when the professor declared that the more we learn the less we actually know. That was a revelation that continues to resonate for me. We began to swim in the tidal drift – the "particular lyrical and existentialist shift that shows one's own drama to be contemplated as if from without" (Italo Calvino). In Camus and Sartre's writings we learnt of the seemingly meaningless struggle – like a dung beetle carrying its life-giving load uphill – in a world that seemed to make little sense and where even a chair, according to Ionesco's plays, was not always necessarily a chair. And in film there was a new realistic wave that would capture blemishes and hardships in sharp focus rather than romancing and whitewashing reality. Or in politics lectures where we learned about percentages of swinging voters, or in economic history where we saw corrupt systems in which we once had faith, or in statistics, where facts were instead *damn lies*.

For my parents, on the other hand, there was probably

enormous satisfaction in a day-by-day existence with security and a predictable rhythm, where life's moves had some rhyme. That might be why, when I took to writing poetry again in later years, my father was a little thrown when he noticed that some of the poems didn't rhyme.

It was my mother who taught me a type of rhyming in the very precise and patterned activity of knitting which in my hands resulted in very short pullovers that barely covered my midriff – no-one talked much about midriffs before then nor since – over cord jeans with appliquéd patches of mushrooms. Did she realise that they might've had something to do with magic mushrooms? That was not the sort of talk we had much at all, except she did realise when there was a marijuana plant on one of the bedroom windowsills in the house, though it didn't really get discussed. It seemed somehow just to slip away in the fog of the undefined folklore of the family. In the psychedelic maze we're being told that despite the haze, this is indeed the *real thing*. But the colours swirl and distract.

Metaphorical Me

Wake up to yourself
Ha do I laugh?
What does that even mean
Who else?
What am I missing here?
See who you are
Who we think you are
And get a grip.
So many metaphors
They pass me by.
I thought I was already real.

Lights Low

Live in the sunshine, swim the sea, drink the wild air.
— Ralph Waldo Emerson

As though she's standing in a dark room trawling through the negatives of a life's snapshots but then in front of her gaze emerges a discernible image. It's my mother's own face, barely distinguishable, but instantly knowable like a stranger in a passing bus from an afternoon in the past. The here and gone, the near and faraway – ourselves, in soft focus.

My father's focus was more on the feathered cut of my brother's hair, or the width of his flared trousers. But fortunately, he was in a secure job at the bank, a much wiser move than being a photographer or a graphic designer, which is where his actual flair seemed to be, but my father was vindicated in his view when the bank did actually provide a lot of security during my brother's long illness.

My mother would silently acquiesce, forever the go-between to mollify family disagreement. She was the arbiter, the mediator, the diplomat in changing times when the dichotomies of outlook such as independence versus anti-authority, progress versus stagnation, seemed to blur in distinction. By adolescence the order of things and faith in them were opened up for closer inspection. And seemed to have fallen into disarray. A son grew his hair too long and wore patterned wide ties. A daughter wore hot pants to wine bars and would traipse off in outsized platform shoes and a skirt too short to inner-city slum places that were once just unsuitable for a date and simply out of bounds.

As adolescents we also resisted some aspects of change, although really they were the beginnings of environmental activism rather than simply rejecting change. Life was good when back at McMasters Beach for the usual sun-bleached summer holiday we rode the waves with the Surf Club crowd. We thrilled to be the first one to shout "Shark!" if we spotted one just beyond the crest of the farthest wave. Then in the evening, with bronzed skin and sun-streaked hair, we would dance at the Surf Club. Later, when some had driving licences, they would cruise around the neighbourhood, ripping down real estate signs out of fear that the place would become over-developed and change our piece of paradise. Even for us, there might have been a question of trying to hang on, or to let go.

The fan reverberated its cooling air across our thoughts and the rhythm of the summer days oscillated in time with the tides, high to low. Up in the sand hills, where we often had played as children, the breeze now breathes through the low-lying branches of the grevillea shrubs along the coast where you would catch the call of wattlebirds as they collected honey.

The voices of my childhood return with faint reminders of all that growing up really meant. Why does it take so long? Why do we not listen out better, and so hear all the messages and make sense of the signs?

The Sandman and Me

The Sandman, a bohemian,
he's in rhapsody when the wind blows
and he drifts in on the sea air,
dusts off the day and lies down;
sand grains blow through the air, turning
to nothing of substance, though everywhere,
like a crumbling sand cake,
they're the particles of dreams drifting lightly,
dreams slipping through his fingers
and he sand-shoe shuffles
his way into my embrace secure,
battened down against the gusts
of uncertainty, against his frailty —
for in the morning he set out
knowing where he was heading
floating free, his sails unfurled on the soft wind
but by evening,
through the thrill of tremolos and trills,
he has stumbled adrift on the drafts and flurries.

Summer Oscillations

The whipbird's call cracks stark
across the dry-leaved silence,
cockatoos' urgent shrills
dare and retreat,
sulphur crests rise with the upsurging waves
while seagulls wheel on the diminuendo.

Ochre dawning with enthusiastic blush
hush and rush, ocean murmurings,
goose bumps and chills,
thrills and summer-fuelled
voices from the beach come in waves,
gentle piano and crashing forte.

Hunched on the seaside she-oak bark
the cicadas drum their cadenza;
close the window on the blast and glare
like the sea's surge now subsiding.
tidal highs to low,
on the summer to and fro draw the blinds down.

Listing sailboat sun-dipped on the beyond,
brilliance and haze, we loll and laze,
stroked by the sun, lulled unthinking
swimmers lilting
moods in syncopated motion
drift on the swirl and calm.

*In the fading light seaweed and shells
contraband on the sand,
blue-bottle sea creatures
evening nor-easter on the salt-spray,
undulating currents, lapping ripples,
deep vermillion triples sun-up to sun-down.
Muffled rumbling of a fan's blades –
oscillating drone, whirring, constant,
tilted to cool wide-gapped toes –
lullabies into sun-drunk dozing;
cloying honeysuckle clings to the air,
scents reverberate.*

*Ebbing undertones, laughing flow,
sounds of solstice revelry
in pillow dishevelry sun-streaked hair,
bronze bangles and candles, gilt-edged pleasures
moon-gleam treasures flicker and fade,
light turned to shade,
time and tide... take the summer-long ride.*

Fragile Faith

Your shadow at morning striding behind you. Or your shadow at evening rising to meet you.
— *The Wasteland,* T.S. Eliot

By now we were holding up the looking glass, and our flimsy shadows confronted us. Our slant on a once rose-coloured world was subverted. Like pom-poms and twinsets and pearls, scrapbooks eventually tended to go the same way – once a sign of treasuring what was significant and of value, now a sign of over-sentimentality and even lack of trust in the safety of technological storage. My brothers and I went to other places via the technology of the day such as walkie-talkies, made from tin cans and string. These morphed into the crystal set and then the transistor radio which we kept under our pillows to listen to faraway voices broadcast across the night.

And so it was with collecting shells. We would come to see the ironic side of that pastime of storing and hoarding, as people put their ears to collected shells so they could believe in the sea whispers, and because their eyes were closed. And rock collections that had been displayed for their mystery and their story of distant places and time, eventually became dust-ridden and discarded. The sfumato of irony washed over our gaze, smudging boundaries and convictions.

Shoehorns and clothes brushes and gadgets to de-pill pullovers – we had faith in these wardrobe artefacts for good grooming – even the use of that word became less entrenched in our vernacular than it had been during daily routines like shoe cleaning with all its own paraphernalia.

And the mirror-fronted medicine cabinet filled with the "just in case" practical salves, lotions and bandages was also central to family interactions. All these practical objects secured our day by day in reassuring ritual and signified my mother's attitude to family matters, always pragmatic, which is why she could treat medical issues thoroughly and unflustered and not convey any fear to us. She had let us maintain a serenity and naïveté which is a child's right, a strong belief of hers. The child with a stray irritating eyelash in the corner of her eye looked to her mother to solve the problem. The ointment was applied, our vision blurred for the moment but the problem was solved.

My mother had also taught us humility and respect for our teachers and others in authority and old age. In a Rolling Stones sort of "out of time" way it was difficult, though, for youth to align their outlook with an older person's life perspective. A schoolgirl's observations reflect the generational mismatch:

> She smiled at us with her widest smile, full of charm and generous spirit. Only we focussed on some spittle that bubbled around her teeth while she spouted words, muted and muffled to the ears of fifteen year old girls. What were teenagers of the sixties to make of that? She was our librarian in what should be a respected place.
>
> Tempting to think of her as a rare book on a dusty shelf, collecting years of whispered

secrets that cobwebbed over in their out-of-dateness. But in her mind she was indeed à la mode and delighted in telling us that she had been a model back in the day. As she expounded the details of the Dewey cataloguing system – which was going to be in the next test – our focus was on her wispy hair, styled into the two buns on each side of her head and set in hairnets that gave them a permanently sculpted look.

She arrived each day at school wearing her fishnet gloves and seamed stockings with black sling-back shoes. She had a tendency to walk on her toes rather than solidly on her whole foot. Maybe it was a reverence for the quiet library space, as if walking normally would destroy an ambience that only she had noticed. Lost on sniggering schoolgirls in their egocentric preoccupations. Or maybe it was a tendon issue from birth or maybe the result of wearing high heels in that disappearing youth of hers, which to our eyes was a closed book.

When she went home each night was she lonely or did she have a lover? No idea. We didn't think about that. Did her home have lots of bookcases filled with books that she seemingly would treasure, or was that a front? Or a stop-gap for what might have been in her life. Might-have-beens – was she one of them?

*A thousand words
Never show their true meaning
Like star points in the sky
Or pictures in our dreaming.*

Off Balance – bickering and bombings

That is longing: To dwell in the flux of things.
— Rainer Maria Rilke

In our early childhood in the 1960s there was a sense of security that things would stay the same and that we were safe. Free milk was one of those entitlements that was reliable and fair. While now we might see it as a political move, then it was seen as making complete sense – milk consumption should equate to protecting children's health and growing healthy bones. We had faith, things were straightforward.

Some of that faith was tested with the abduction and murder of an eight year old boy in Sydney. It was thought to be the first kidnapping for ransom case in Australia. His parents had recently won the lottery which had been set up to help with the escalating financial shortfall for building the Opera House. It might be seen as a time when Australia lost its innocence. We can picture a young child listening to the story on the wireless radio in fear and a pet dog to protect and reassure now posted outside the bedroom window. And our mothers, tracking their children's safety en route to school, hiding behind shopfronts so as not to give the children the same fear of something menacing. Three years later, with the assassination of President John F. Kennedy, there was a further sense that world order had changed.

We could say that Australian life had an ease and freedom. Seeing ourselves as the lucky country, the title of Donald Horne's book written in 1964, we put faith in our rich resources and lived life with the assumption so often expressed in everyday talk that "she'll be right Mate" – it went hand-in-hand with not complaining about things, we just got on with the job. Many liked to think that it was part of the Australian identity – we had little sense of questioning what Australian identity actually meant, if it could even exist. In any case, never as children and adolescents did we see our parents show any frailties or uncertainty, almost like black and white cardboard cut-outs of themselves.

Kilter and Karma

How is it that the healer isn't healed?
Her soft tears glisten with the truth.
How is it that the yogi is off-balance?
Her mood swings reveal her dizziness of spirit.
The teacher who knows things has lost command
As she can't seem to be sure enough to say.
The businessman prevaricates
As though there may be another view.
And the athlete with torn ligaments
Relapses reluctantly into a slowed gait.

Relying on memory, itself a reconstruction, and getting to the truth of any matter, seems to take us on a silent, crooked and sometimes obscured path. And how hard is it to understand the everyday when it is filled with bickering and bombings and outrage encapsulated in news footage and songs like the 1965 Good News Week song: ... *someone's dropped a bomb somewhere, contaminating atmosphere, and blackening the sky.* Disruption or upheaval was itself a new way of viewing the world requiring faith in uncertainty and catching existentialist time before it passed us by.

For many, the refrain, *What's the weather like today?* remained the more important question. My parents, and the nation generally, had their own version of naïveté – the one of putting faith in rules and regulations and tidy houses with mown lawns, in banking institutions, in health care and insurance, in political leaders of a particular party – because that's what families did and because we hadn't yet thought enough about the possible oxymoron of *honest politician*. But where did those chiaroscuro certainties go when times changed? Understanding retracted to the shadows. With student uprisings, feminist marches and anti-colonial protests, things were no longer as they had seemed.

Naïveté and Nuances

It's a poor sort of memory that only works backward.
— *Alice in Wonderland,* Lewis Carroll

And so the challenge is to see how memory can work forwards and be with us in the present — how is it still relevant? Childhood memories tend not to go away, we must make of them what we can. Then again perhaps, as the Duchess declared in Lewis Carroll's *Alice in Wonderland,* "It's no use going back to yesterday because I was a different person then."

That same sort of feeling as a child who has fallen off the seesaw, flat hard onto the ground but trying not to show how much it actually hurt, for fear of admitting to being inept at something supposedly easy. That was the embarrassment and awkwardness of a child, red-cheeked and off-balance. That was naïveté. Like the time when the great aunts from the Central Coast — one a school librarian and one a dance instructor — paid us a visit at the McMasters Beach cottage. When they arrived, we were standing outside avoiding the ants and the heat of the sand, next to us the water tanks and the washing line, further up the slope, the outside dunny — not a place for lingering.

I spoke up when the aunts asked me how the holidays were going and had I been enjoying school. When I replied, all positive, the whole group of adults laughed at something I said. I didn't actually know what it was. Maybe it was optimism itself, which is why I was approvingly patted on the head.

But soon enough, as long summer naïveté faded, it was time to see through our romanticised Zorro days and see things as they were. It was time to face up to the fact that dark-masked Zorro riding his stallion with its brushed shiny flanks was just a man whose sword could strip our pale thin clouds of delusion to shreds. And the world in our mind's windmills is "like an apple whirling silently in space" (Noel Harrison), where the moon has had its beaming face trodden on. It was time to move on from naïveté.

Moon-faced dawn

I looked out to sea, at first light
as owls and nightingales hid from sight,
the tune of their wise and sad songs
to the faraway belongs,
and there was your rippled face
seemingly out of place
in a watery disguise,
across sepia-washed skies;
was it a frown or a stare
did you offer the dare –
shun the darkest fearful night
and brave the birdman's flight.

Psyche

We had dead butterflies
splattered all over
the windscreen –
butterflies and butterflies
sheer surrender
to times and tribulations
beyond their comprehension,
soft wing cataclysm
on shatter-proof glass
a black spotted convulsion of wings
the wanderer searching
orange flutter
shuttered in the day bright
pauses for nectaring
mid-migration
from somewhere to somewhere
for some reason
we don't know or understand,
except they have to do it
and then they'll be gone
having played some part
ripple on ripple
fractured, making no sense
in our own world
in its irreverence.

Icons and Incongruities

Between the idea and the reality falls the shadow.
— T.S. Eliot

Had we stopped to think what kept our mothers and fathers awake through all those hours, when ghosts become real, and insinuate their icy limbs through our tossed blankets, and their thin fingers sort through the mess of our mind's frayed tangle. Like taking the brush to the knots of a dishevelled sleepy head of hair, in the telling of facts and impressions of the past, some complexities of human dreams and nightmares might be teased out. But between dreams and awakening uncertain shadows loom.

Our world moved into an iconoclastic era – the sacrosanct was no longer. Rules were broken. The Red Cross, for example, had previously been out of bounds as bomb targets, but that changed in World War II – my mother was still outraged thirty years later. Look what happens when order is taken out of where it belongs. The result – violence, greed, war, disease, anti-authoritarianism – such difficult concepts to grasp when the status quo shifts. There was the slow realisation that disorder was the new truth and a more nuanced outlook replaced certainty.

My parents, however, also had a certain cynicism about the incongruous, and even an inverse snobbery sometimes, as when my father described success in the office as getting to sit at the desk in the first row. This was not unlike the 1962 song by Malvina Reynolds that they liked, where people all lived in little boxes that were all the same, they all did the same things and they all look the same, and their children turned out the same. Those little boxes were made of ticky-tacky – inferior quality – not at all like the double brick that was so dependable. Lack of dependability is echoed in today's failure to comply with rules as heard in the media stories of corrupt bank cultures, of falsified documents, stealing from the accounts of the deceased, of fake news, of the hollow men, of a world that might end not with a bang but a tweet.

Reflections within reflections – can they meet and see eye-to-eye? Do we see each other within ourselves and so more easily co-exist? This reminiscing feels like cocoon-building, it shelters and nurtures at the same time. It pulls apart incongruities of the past but doesn't necessarily resolve them.

It seems that growing up was like being in a room of curiosities. Curiouser and curiouser... all is not what it seemed, there was the putting together of parts of creatures that don't go together – like the dodo disguised as a croquet mallet in Lewis Carroll's *Alice in Wonderland*. At the front door of my house I'm imagining now the feel of the door handle in my tightened palm. It has opened in my mind a closed off world. It's as inviting as the smell of tealeaves in the teapot. I hadn't known where the doorway would lead. But I found out more than I thought possible. There were swans with the webbed feet of monsters, there were marmots with platypus bills. Incongruities co-existed. I had never noticed in the wonderland of childhood that tortoise head coming out of the wall just below a wooden cross. Another tortoise is flying. Just below is the bold peacock seemingly oblivious to the man in purple tights with a hunting gun and binoculars stepping towards the window. At his wrist there is his lace cuff and a giant starfish on the shelf. And just above his head on the wall an aardvark face-to-face with a mongoose leering at the miniature sailboat. Things that don't match force our attention. Why weren't we listening? Why weren't we seeing? But outside of books, those things were never visible. In the adult world, viewed from adolescent eyes, the creativity embraced in the corners of childhood was absent in day-by-day living. And we recall T.S. Eliot's message: "Where is the Life we have lost in living?"

> *The butterfly set sail*
> *alone –*
> *alone on the sea*
> *she wing-tipped the tide turning*
> *and danced with the anemone.*

Grace, Gratitude and Grit

Gratitude makes sense of past, peace for today and creates a vision for tomorrow.

— Melody Beattie

How we choose to respond – and we do choose – to what we are given in life is what makes us unique. Or even whether we believe in that choice of the word *given* which indicates a stance, because it is hard to reign things to within our control. When you think about it, both gratitude and wonder can only be your own, of your own making. Others have suffered, each has her burden. The poignancy of our situation comes from our own response to it, no more, no less real than that of another. As Montaigne urged in loving life and its beauty, the particular task is "to know how to enjoy those blessings with temperance and to lose them with fortitude".

Grace is the willow low-leaning, leaf-shaped tears shed and reformed, a triumphant-green renewal. Or perhaps it's just as the words on a local billboard might read with the quotable quotation of the day: "Accept what is, let go of what was and have faith in what will be." My mother, with her sense of wonder and of gratitude, I tend to see as a woman of grace.

Woman – a hard hat and a lipstick

Not long out of bed she's putting on her lipstick,
a kind of coral colour,
not with any sense of irony,
an image of sunny luxuriance ... she just likes it ...
Or is it a subservience to others' desires not hers?
To assumed sexuality, preconceived images -
what should be,
a bright persona with no out-of-place melancholy.

It's the little emblem she keeps in her purse,
an ever-ready tool
to show she's in control ... or not.
She re-applies and smiles back ... you see it works,
she smiles at herself in the looking glass.
It brings out her best, some class, shows she bothers.

Later on when it's faded off her lips
she will think again about what the image is.
Can't seem to make up her mind.
She bends to put on her steel-capped boots,
ties the laces with a firm hand, puts on a smirk,
opens the heavy front door and heads to work.

Her hard hat under her arm
she strides beside the flame tree –
there's that same coral colour –
an intense glare on her thoughts;
the purple of the jacaranda overfills her gaze-
open-eyed passion to assert her will, to be herself.

The hard hat is her uniform and her protection,
The lipstick is her expression, a mere symbol –
coquettish coral character – exotic and beyond...
But somehow they define her in these grey streets.
Yet the questions remain the same,
"Who is she"? "What is she"? Does it have a name?

Even in the word "she" written in lipstick
On the mirror, there would be just one letter
distinguishing "he" and "she"
So what does that show – minor detail in theory
but not the reality.
She strides down the street and onto the building site
To take up position for a hard day's work,
As good as the rest of them ... only different.

Turning Tide

Nous vivons dans un arc-en-ciel de chaos. (We live in a rainbow of chaos.)

— Paul Cézanne

> *Time and tide wait*
>
> *For no fool*
> *too slow to see it coming.*
> *White horses gallop*
> *on the cresting wave*
> *gambolling on the froth and bubble*
> *hard-hooved, relentless*
> *they trample*
> *on the fallen*
> *in the way*
> *of the high and low,*
> *immutable flow,*
> *they drown in their doubt.*

The glaring colour of the red sail-boat has been brush-stroked against the still lapis lazuli sea and the cascades of yellow cassia-like blobs of paint, stretch down the ochre cliffs that loom high above. My mother surely wanted the opportunity to set sail and do what she wanted to do, to travel, to be a teacher, to raise a family and see them go safely out into their own worlds, only not too far from the shoreline. The waves recede, you walk farther out on the shore, taking a higher and higher risk. Whether staying on the clifftop or setting sail, things happen that make us change tack but what do we make of that? Or perhaps it is a question of being becalmed in the falling light. Caught in a hiatus, we catch the beauty we see in the shards of light, the shimmers and sighs from now-fading days. And moon-winks restless time.

Perhaps, apart from fading eyesight, that was why ageing parents gravitated towards brighter hues as if muted palettes might make their very selves fade into an impressionist background where they had no hold in an autumn light and no real definition, where memories as well as appearances became hazy.

Lighthouse

Keeping watch,
it's lonely lens
on the faraway,
forever and a day,
white sails unfurled.

We weren't playing cockylora ball games anymore or cricket in the backyard. It had them stumped though. What do you do when the child says no? What do you do when the music talks of love and war with irony? No, things were never the same, never as they had seemed. And it had been my mother's role to make it look as though they were. That's why apple pie was so important. That's why days of the week had a ritual. That was why hydrangeas in rows were earnestly tended. Things that mattered. How did my mother know that already? She hadn't even read Voltaire's *Candide* who told us about the importance of cultivating a garden to sustain us.

That was why we had always done one thing at a time – start Brownies at six years old, tennis at eleven, tennis club at fifteen because it's a "good social game", as long as you met people like yourself – as it happened, it was on the courts that I met my husband-to-be, George. A marvellous thing is a mother's determination, manoeuvring the best for her child. That is why, for the sake of measured certainty, the hard-backed dictionary was prominent in our family home, and encyclopaedias were the word. And that is why I keep my father's Latin grammar school primer.

Since when did concrete paths give way?

Stepping onto a concrete square in full stride
on a morning walk,
the rickety block unnerved my sense of certainty
that such things were to be counted on
but this has been the long slow meander
to realising that nothing is forever
and nothing is for sure,
ever since Ionesco and other thinkers
told me with oblique wording that
a chair is not a chair
and now I know that the ground we stand on
shifts.

Coffee Cacophony

Is it the friendship or is it the bean,
Joie de vivre or perhaps the caffeine?
In robust haste consumers come and go
Keen for single-origin espresso.
Enter into anonymous clatter,
Come together to flatter and chatter.
Immersed in humanity's extra-hot flow.
Seeking a fine-tuned skinny piccolo,
They whisper over a laughing latte,
Exchange secrets and pungent repartee.
You can hear the playful innuendo,
Imbibe a full-bodied cappuccino.
No-point decaf or Arabica brew
Volatile debate – is that true, who knew?
Was that really a fervid crescendo
Or the buzz of mature macchiato?
On the scene are the artful baristas,
In come cruising the smooth-bearded hipsters,
For now they chill with an affogato,
Today's fast fads soon to become retro.
They chase their leisure in peopled surrounds
Humming in reverence for hallowed grounds.

From Hula Hoops to Hipsters

Have you heard the latest hipster joke? Wait I have it here somewhere on vinyl ...

— David Astle

Enter into that disrupted scene, the hipster full of retro and reality, and you know the *too cool to clean the tables vibe* from the waiters, and the hedging-my-bets coffee order for an almond milk double shot latte with Manuka honey. As I record these recollections I'm thinking of the advice to writers from DBC Pierre: "Write in a reckless fever. Rewrite in a cardigan". The cardigan was hard to escape in the fifties and sixties. It was the infinitely sensible garment of choice for accountants and for women to cover their arms for the sake of modesty or for the change of temperature – obligatory for children when dusk fell and mothers feeling the cold would call them in from play. This was another means of regulating our lives – the control of the thermostats of our days. And now the cardigan has returned, adopted by hipsters and fashionistas in oversized proportions to make a statement of comfort and retrospective style.

And the vinyl was no longer playing for my mother – the tunes were too different. In the wings my mother had watched her teenage daughter manouevre her way through relationships and high school and higher education. In the wings she would be silently willing me to succeed. Though I rarely heard her. Many parents in the seventies might have cried John Lennon's words, *nobody told me* what was going on. And still the cry echoes through to today as times change – feeling out of sync with the times, *strange days indeed.* Vicissitudes and vexations became the new tune.

This must surely have been what my mother was hearing as her children grew up and changed. Not that she had wanted to hold us too tight. Only that she needed to understand. In those changing times a visualisation of a mother-daughter interaction and the comings and goings of boyfriends might go something like this:

> The mother answers the telephone on the first ring. She frowns and hands it to her daughter without a word. She knows it must be him. The daughter takes her time to get there. Out the window the sun's rays much lower in the sky now, casting dim shadows on the floorboards. Do I really want to talk? she thinks. That same spiral of uncertainty, between tension and reason, heart and mind, endless and wearying, where's the joy in that?
>
> In his first gentle words on the end of the line, she listens in and then lets herself wander to thoughts of something else. She closes her eyes. Her mother has gone back to rolling out pastry. Such an on-the-ground thing to be doing, an unquestioning approach; she has a good feel for how the short pastry should be – the memorised recipe, tried and true, it's her guide to success.
>
> Then there's the Leonard Cohen song sounding over and over again: A man never got a woman back by begging on his knees.

Howling at the moon wouldn't work. He's got to prove his worth. How come she knew that?

The soft voice continues at the other end, but something in the pastry rolling routine switched off the desire button and turned on common sense. Then again, doesn't everyone want the moon howling? That's the yearning, the somewhere else, far from here. Her resolve is slowly melting in the now dark evening in MacArthur Park, a musical skyrocket shot through the collective longings. So we're not alone in seeking out what else there is or are there in fact lonely Eleanor Rigbies everywhere? They listen long for the knock at the door or the sound of the telephone ringing. Where, indeed, do they all belong?

Womansong

Like a cicada
I have come out of the dark
to find my voice,
now shrill with the effort
it takes to beat my message loud and clear.
Leave the window open – I want my voice heard,
not loudly, just at normal volume
but I keep having to turn it up.

*How is it that my own tune
is less valued than a man's?
Why have you not listened
to your daughter, your mother, your grandmother?
Does their place in the world not make you realise
that they have formed who you are.
How is it that you can be indifferent
to the plight of those treated as less than equal?*

*Everyday instant news and reporting
can omit the slower process of empathy,
true listening, obscure though that can be –
"What seems other is not other at all
but just us on a different day".
Let's now choose a different day
so that you might then say to me,
you should sing your song and we'll now listen.*

*When drivers overtake us at too-high speed
we apply our own brakes to let them forge ahead.
I am Frida Kahlo. I am Camille Claudel. Our art has
been our song. I am a housewife, an office worker,
a starlet, a child bride, an athlete –
we all have our tunes to play.
Most of all, I am.
Therefore I have the right to voice who I am.*

*But not at the expense of another.
This is not a question of opening the door for me.
Every time you say to me I cannot pay you the same
every time you look away from me*

*because I don't appeal to your ego
and every time you keep me waiting in line
to compete with those who have louder voices,
you are telling me I am not worthy.*

*I'm just asking to have my voice heard,
having waited in the dark wings too long.
Have I not earned the right to sing,
whether for my supper or my super
or just to have my say?
Open the window – don't crush the cicada crescendo.
Can you tell me when you will listen
Sincerely, Everywoman.*

Flux

What we are today comes from our thoughts of yesterday,
and our present thoughts build our life of tomorrow.
Our life is the creation of our mind.

— Buddha

So ours was the time of the gaping generation gap – the suspended blue hour has drifted into the suspended days of misunderstanding, new incongruities as old and new coincide in a blur of co-existence. Now faster than ever, it takes a while to realise that the flurried state won't go away. That flux is life itself, its to and fro.

Our childhood neighbour wrote to me a couple of years back and told me that a substantial two-storey building, had replaced our family home – leaving very little space for a garden "which reminds me how much Heather loved hers and the floral art demonstrations she conducted. So many memories flooding in."

And so we have tears for days gone by and for a world no longer there. There are scars that we could pick at and make raw and heal them with Mercurochrome, calamine lotion, band aids, Dettol antiseptic and aspirin crushed in condensed milk ... simple remedies for childhood scrapes but none of these would ever be useful against disease and dying days that were bigger than all of us.

In much later years whenever I went to visit my parents my mother would usually say, "Well what's news?" I realised I was it and felt obliged to amplify the parts of my recent couple of days that to me seemed ordinary with more of that sobriety and significance of the old black and white newsreels. But to them it meant a different world from their own day by day. I needed to create occasion and drama, I needed to tell them stories to take them away. My mother would eagerly wait for some titbit of information as though she were isolated from the world and I was the higgledy piggledy bridge that would somehow save them from too much of themselves. The to and fro of conversation though was so often unenlightening on either side. We were simply dutifully pouring tea and organising the shrunken world of the elderly so that they could live their days more easily.

Now I've stopped pushing back – glad they liked the poets I hadn't but now do, I am glad they embraced their music and their dancing, and those flowers and birds and posies, worlds in miniature and maps … and those humble holidays and scrap books and photo albums – lest we forget.

Missed you

I've been in a mist of memories
Unending.
Across the seas and beyond,
A longing that lasts too long
Dispelled by a homecoming,
No more bound by tightened threads
No more might have beens
The spell unspooled.

Aspro and Lymphoma, Hiccups and Oesophaguses

… in a mother's life there's a promise at dawn it never keeps.
— *The Promise of Dawn*, Romain Gary

Dangerous diseases, hushed tones, the light dimmed down on the day by day as her second-born son lay dying. It struck in those years when children are no longer children but are on the brink of opportunity, just twenty years of age. How strong she was as she spent hours and hours on hospital visits, months and months tending to her son's needs; hours in the specialists' rooms and in the ward, confused as to how lymphoma was not something they could fix. Shocked that there could be no hope at all. And then overjoyed when he had a brief reprieve and went surfing up the coast. Until it all came back in a tide that left desolate souls on its shore.

Graham again became seriously ill and was fighting to survive cancer. On one of the days when he felt he had enough energy, he set off up the Lane Cove River in his small runabout cruiser that our parents had bought so he could cast off and be free in a way that illness does not allow. He moved along the smooth sheltered waters, past the mangrove mudflats where crabs clambered among the tuber roots. It was where we had gone crabbing with my father years before, dredging them up out of the mud to use for bait.

Only a little farther along the river the engine failed which meant that to get back home Graham had to paddle with one oar for a few kilometres. Already feeble from his illness, he finally made it back, exhausted and deflated in spirit. The truth of casting off as free as a pirate had now been swapped for the truth of needing to stay on the shore.

And so began the downward draining of hope and certainty. I recall the time when my father was calling over the fence to Max, the surgeon next door. My father would not ordinarily have done that because the neighbour was perceived as being not very good at telling his children to stop throwing things, like cans and wrappers, into our yard. And he had a habit of singing operatically, very loudly in a way that intruded on the privacy of our family next-door mental space. But here we are. My mother can't catch her breath, it was lost when the telephone rang and we learnt that my brother was not doing well in hospital, they weren't hopeful. My mother's breathing is more and more laboured, more and more extreme gasps. She might pass out. Max might be able to fix it. He comes into our living room and gently asks my mother to blow into a brown paper bag – the kind my mother had always put our school lunches in, those warm Vegemite sandwiches that as a teenager I'd thrown into the bin. My mother listens to Max and responds to his calm approach. Quietly her breathing becomes easy. Quietly she apologises for causing a fuss. Quietly she wants time to come back to herself. I don't think she ever did.

Graham did return home but continued to deteriorate until on his very final day he went back to the hospital. The saddest sound is when there's no sound at all from the ambulance, the siren is turned off, there's no longer any urgency.

My mother had lost the most precious gift from her own life and from then on it kept her inside of herself and she remained in a slow-motion haze. She adored her five grandchildren and revelled in keeping alive for them what she had done for us – sparking their imaginations and encouraging their learning and their swimming. She and my father in his retirement started taking trips to sunnier parts of Australia to escape Sydney's winter and breathe in some comfort from nature. Her own body slowed down and the pain in her spirit was also outward pain in all her arthritic limbs.

But many years earlier, when her first son John was a very young child, she had sat in a darkened room, keeping watch, with a look as tender as silk, she saw him come close to death with childhood measles, then potentially fatal and now immunised away. He survived, lived happy days as a child and carved out in adulthood what he wanted. Seemingly with his feet on the ground and his father's skills at building what he needed in his home, he still constantly seemed to have a restless concern that maybe this is all there is. Nearly fifty years into his life his mother couldn't keep the same vigil for him as she had for him as a child. It would no longer be possible to simply give him a glass of water as she did for the then out of control but funny hiccups. Now, with uncontrollable oesophageal cancer, he faded from her forever.

Hush

The infinite tenderness of a brother's kiss
That barely touched the cheek
And the heartstrings
That played the hushed melodies of childhood.
The gone forever strains of joy and wide smiles
The still reverberating refrain
Of laughter and salty tears
Of surprise and fears.
The to and fro of the years'
Meaning and stilled moments,
Slumber and walking hours
One flow of fantasy
That makes sense of the not here
That shapes the want to be
And guides the humming
Of the heart's cacophany.
Echoes issue from a lost source
Sonorous and sustained,
Tugs on sleeves of worn out favourites
The lapping of dreamed whispers.
The threads that hung tattered
From the coat's fleece
That shelters from the discord
Of the absent gaze.

Then as if my mother might still have more tears left in the well for more grieving, the oldest grandchild, Victoria – her grandmother's middle name and the name of her great-grandmother – was in a car accident and was wrenched away from life. This was the blond-curled, soft-skinned child they had played with in her home in Byron Bay. Then as a young woman, on the brink of exploring beyond, she was gone.

Tragedies are always one's own – others cannot take the pain on their own shoulders. Yet across the world still there are many hunched shoulders pulled tight to protect against the blows of the realities of sad lives or hard lives. We try to put our hands up to shield us from the glare when the light is too bright, it hurts our eyes to see what we wished was still a blur. While my mother's tragedies do not define her, they became etched into the soft-shaded outline of her profile.

Shivering – what is it?

It's when there's a change in the air
Like an involuntary dare,
No longer in control,
Like a puppeteer's stare-eyed doll;
Or a shift in the status quo:
Is it stemming the sanguine flow?
Or a primeval flood
Of reptilian blood
In our veins and thin skin
Alert awakening... frisson of frozen fright.

Lights out, wide-eyed game begun
After early-setting pale sun
As children we quivered in winter's dark
On haunches crouching, silence stark,
Huddled with scarcely a breath,
Pre-emptive play at cheating death:
The steam from our stopped mouths
Is cold-packed with suspense,
Our pounding pulse immense,
Rigid fists and clenched jaws,
Irresistible pause...
Full force of our frailty.

But now it's a different theatrical,
Our playing blind and impractical,
The work of a new impresario
On an unimagined scenario:
You take her from the ward
And put her under Damocles sword,
Blunt instruments of frozen propriety
Cutting into cold anxiety
With iced incision,
Cool-fingered prods of precision;
Anaesthetic falling, one ... two ... three,
Lights out, they cannot see her shivering.

Time traveller and Time-pieces

We shall not cease from exploration, and the end of all our exploring will be to arrive where we started and know the place for the first time.

— T.S. Eliot

Relating vignettes from my mother's life, I've stepped around some uncertainties, I've tiptoed over difficulties, I've gone striding through the joys, the timeless emotions given up by a different time and place. Time travelling is what I have done – the ultimate mysterious adventure, the disordering of time and place, of there and then.

Time-keeping must have been significant in the thinking of my great grandmother, on my mother's side. She would give every child in the family at the age of seven a wrist watch, an old lady's gift of a timepiece as if she were watching her time running out – the last little sand grains were slipping through the thin neck of her very own hourglass. The watch she gave me had a round, clear white face with silver numbers and a black, thin looped band – I still have it, still it keeps time; straightforward and understated, something of substance as if she were saying, "Keep an eye on the time … it goes".

It was my mother, though, who travelled back in time more and more. I see her as the actual time traveller. How fitting an activity in the verdigris debris of our winter days. As if here and now were no longer enough, as if she could not let go of what had come before because that was who she was. But she was not that person now so much. Like the hermit characters she might have seen in the outback, she would sometimes close herself in, her fading hearing blocking out the here and now. And besides, perhaps we really are "just a bundle of habits shaped by our memories" (Joshua Foer). With the very early stages of the time-lapse of dementia, she would constantly replay the same songs from the same tracks of the record in her mind. She became stuck on a tune from the long-playing vinyl record of her life, which she kept out of its faded brown dusty jacket and constantly played. Mostly they gave her pleasure to recall.

What freedom, all thanks to the imagination, our mind's eye – "I can see the ocean," she might say, "I can see the orchard at my grandmother's home. I can see my grandchildren slurping on their home-made passionfruit ice blocks." Even now I can hear the smile in her voice. I can imagine her saying, "I'm there but not because I'm here." Clever really, because you don't have to go anywhere. You can sit in your armchair that welcomes spirit and body into its reclining folds and wander wherever your thoughts allow.

And there she was

Smiling to be
untying the bowlines,
released from her moorings
heather-laden,
a mind far-seeing
the near and the gone.

Even now I can see her standing waist-high in the ultramarine sea of lupins and lobelia, silent bold splodges impressed on her heart as she gazes across the pointillist canvas and outside of the frame. And so she achieved the effects of travelling, as in the words of philosopher Alain de Botton, "we may feel we have been returned to ourselves ... brought back into contact with emotions and ideas of importance to us".

The charm in her smile that she had until her last day showed me that "happiness cannot be travelled to, owned, earned, worn, consumed" (Melody Beattie). Happiness is already there within us, you just have to play it. Certainly, there were very sad songs in their lives that would never turn down their haunting sounds but they have their own solace. For my parents it was a marriage of rich and poor, for richer and for poorer, and they made it work. Steadfast always, my mother died two years after my father in the year of what would have been their 70th wedding anniversary.

Grief ball

I'm just a big ball of grief.
I try to flick off its lint
From my shoulders
Lead heavy with the weight
The matted ravelling of my heart string
Drags down my coat pocket
Filled with sad illusions,

Frail fibres of yesterday.
A strand of your hair
Catches in my wedding ring.
Détritus from under my collar
Turned up against the anxious wind
Cluttering, congesting
Can hardly breathe.
It's closing in, constricted
And the fun park shrieks carry across the water
The joy-ride in circular motion
Counters my lurching thoughts
That scatter outwards and inwards
And dodgem back and forth
Choking in the vortex.

In closing up the book of snapshots from my mother's life, the words of Thoreau echo: "There is no other land, there is no other life but this. That is our dilemma to prove this true or to have faith that it is not." Was that the dilemma of my mother and all of her generation and of the generation before them and after them? Or is that my reflection on her life as lived? A reflection within a reflection.

To me, as my mother's child, many of my observations here used not to be especially obvious. And that is the way of the memoir, especially when not completely one's own but told on behalf of another, the telling reconfigures a life lived. Perhaps it helps explain why for me, the child turned adult, there has always been an urge to do more, to imagine more, and in telling these memories I am even more mindful of Thoreau's words: "You must live in the present, launch yourself on every wave, find your eternity in each moment."

So now I'm just slipping out for a walk, I want to breathe in the skies. I want to keep my heart beating strongly, I want to confide in the air that surrounds, to be in the waves and pick the brains of the passing seagull. I see again in my mind's eye, the glow of the sail in white titanium tint, lit up in the light of the sun, out on the wide eternal sea but returning to safe harbour. I'll leave the door ajar, you can leave your tea, you might come too and anyway I'll need to get back inside. She's gone… she forgot to tell me where.

Then and Now

Now that you're gone you make more sense
Why did it take so long to assemble the pieces?
I saw your photo in the drawer.
You were dancing, smiling, whirling in sync
Together.
It reminds me of what I didn't know
Nor want to see.

The waves of swollen memories of my mother and her life fall through my own and land me back, more secure on the shore, and more exhilarated from having taken the ride. I have had my eyes open underwater where at times the vision is blurry and salt-washed and soft-focussed. As I surface, my perspective has gone from a childhood one to an adult view. I want to hear the old songs, the notes in minor key fill my listening ears. Finally, I am looking at them as people who lived as they could in the circumstances they had in the way they thought best, fearful of leaving the shore, yet with a hankering that they filled by getting on with the here and now. They danced in concentric surf-green circles, ever narrowing, but allowing a glance over the shoulder, out the window, onto a sailing boat resting in the blue shallows of the water rippling on the sandy grit of the shore.

Again I think of the image of the silhouetted nuns as they filed across the sand dunes, almost in a mirage, a sleight of vision, their own faith leading to an oasis on the shore. I didn't know that my mother would be seeking her own oasis. And scratching to decipher her own Sanskrit in the sand. I see the spindrift of the years, the sandman impressions blown off the dunes. These tales have seen the rise and fall of laughs rushing in while the tears filled with sapphires and grit are trickling out to sea, the sum of fragments of her life but not the whole sum.

Prism vision

Refractons
rainbow reflections
resurrections of recollections –
are they real?

As the child, it only really became clear to me in my mother's last couple of years, just how close she was to my father, and how co-dependent they became. She had come to rely so much on him for all that had previously been her domain in the household. But at my father's side when he was ill, her determined spirit and her compassion were still clear. I saw this as she leant over his hospital bed in his last few days and stroked his hair. Somehow from within herself she had rustled up her courage and her innate sense of nurturing. And he said how wonderful it was to see her.

There in that scene that I witnessed, they had come the full circle – the heart carved out of shale by a seventeen year old alone in a country town was just as relevant now as it had been all those years before. Indeed, as in T.S. Eliot's words, "the end is where we start from". All that they had seen and endured and shared, or not shared with each other and with their children, was distilled to this. And so I put down her crystal-backed mirror that lit up a reflection within a reflection, the circle has come to a still point within a circle, a memoir within a memoir closes.

How often does that dove coo?

It's an untimed repetition,
a long meek chiming of the hours
of the years,
of times gone
but still here at a house
that has heard the timeless call –
solid as the cut blocks of sandstone

edged with lichen,
a dove-grey disguise of storied memories.
Past the slate linen draped at the window
with its brushed-silver handle
I see the hand-chiselled stone wall
at the edge of the garden,
the red poppies flimsy-petalled
vivid in their statement,
in their stance unsure of what has been
or will return.
The wisteria leaves lean
 across the iron gate
with its rusty-edged lock
and I can wander with my eyes
to the secluded garden beyond,
a hideaway from voices,
and footsteps on the crushed gravel,
its crunch is here and now.
And back at my window desk
the clouds reflected in its glass
rush past with the white haze of the moment
where I'm cocooned in a serene place.
And still the dove coos.

Gone sailing

Sail on and when it's done
The voyage has just begun.
When the tear begins, it has already fallen
In the waking dreaming
There is the end.

www.ingramcontent.com/pod-product-compliance
Lightning Source LLC
Chambersburg PA
CBHW032029170426
43195CB00047B/773